A Human's Guide To

Dog Toilet Troubles

A Human's Guide To

Dog Toilet Troubles

All canine pee & poo problems resolved

Marilyn Peters & Klea Morianou

ANIMINDS BOOKS

ISBN - 9798605571391

Acknowledgments

This book would not have been possible without the help and support of several people. Our sincere thanks and appreciation for the generous support during this project go to: Nicholas Rossis for planting the idea of indie-writing and self-publishing, Vangelis Karatzas (defrost-design.gr) for the cover and the book design, Dimi Xepapadeas for editing most of the imperfections and the Noun Project (thenounproject.com) for helping us visually spice up our book with their royalty-free icons library.

Most importantly, a massive thanks to you for investing in our book. We hope you enjoy reading it and find our book helpful.

CONTENTS

13

14

A HUMAN'S GUIDE TO DOG TOILET TROUBLES

About this book and its use

Dog toilet troubles? What an odd subject for a book! We thought so too in the beginning. However, owing to the fact that we were both rehabilitating all kinds of different dogs, and were, by that point, waist deep in various different kinds of pee and poo problems, we realised that something wasn't right. It was not natural for this many humans to be having all these soiling problems with their dogs. After all, proper soiling behaviour is, or should be for that matter, the first thing that dogs learn during their journey with us.

Something was definitely amiss because our lives, as canine professionals, had literally been taken over by canine toilet problems! What was happening? We hit the books to figure things out and quickly realised, in shock, that there was no one book that dealt purely and thoroughly with this topic; a book that covered pee and poo from A to Z; a book that started in puppyhood and ended in adulthood, with rehabilitation tips and advice for toilet-related behavioural problems. This needed to change—and fast. We thereby made it our mission to open Pandora's box and talk extensively about what seems to be a taboo subject, and to do it without remorse. Pee and poo has now become a casual daily topic of discussion for us!

So what is this "pee and poo" book all about? "A Human's Guide to Dog Toilet Troubles" is a compilation of 15 years of behavioural experience on canine toilet-related behavioural issues. It aims to provide complete pee and poo guidance for all dog lovers—dog guardians and professionals alike—and can be used in several ways; as a practical guide, a textbook, a casual read or merely a reference book.

By reading this book you will become fully equipped with the knowledge on how to successfully:
- housebreak a puppy or adult dog
- prevent canine toilet related behaviour issues
- understand, assess, and ultimately solve canine toilet-related behaviour issues.

As a practical guide for dogs already exhibiting toilet problems, it might help to first check out the 'Self-diagnosis flow chart' in Appendix B LINK. It will give you a way to pinpoint the probable cause, or causes, of your dog's problem, thus making whatever kind of toilet trouble you are facing clearer. Once you know the underlying cause—for example, whether your dog is exhibiting submissive urination, separation anxiety or is simply marking—then you can direct yourself to the relevant paragraphs in 'Chapter 6: Causes of adult toilet trouble' for specific information regarding your canine companion's actual behaviour and ways to overcome it.

Dogs are failing miserably to meet human expectations with regard to toilet etiquette but not due to any shortcomings on the dogs' part. More often than not, humans are lacking the know-how of properly communicating their expectations to their four-legged friends, often generating a lot of confusion and stress in the process. As a result, inappropriate soiling is a big problem for humans but an even bigger one for dogs who often end up abandoned in shelters where many are euthanized if they can't be rehomed.

The difference between pee and poo

Before starting your read, it is important to highlight a minor discrepancy between peeing and pooing. Within this book, when referring to soiling, we usually mean both pee and poo, especially when discussing house-breaking training, whether for puppies or adult dogs. We train for both pee and poo in exactly the same way. Nothing changes. Differences start when talking about soiling-related problem behaviour in adolescent and adult dogs for reasons that will be outlined below. It is for these reasons that more emphasis is given to pee-ing, since behavioural soiling problems usually mani-fest with pee rather than poo. Poo will usually be a re-sult of either a medical problem or a fear/anxiety-re-lated behavioural problem, like separation anxiety.

Pee and poo are waste by-products of two different organ systems. Pee originates from the urinary system and poo from the digestive system. They differ mainly in consistency and quantity. Some important infor-mation about soiling behaviour follows:

Frequency: Dogs pee more often during the day. They may poo only three to four times per day as puppies and one to two times as adults, so it is usually eas-ier to fully housetrain for poo than for pee.

Control: Dogs can control the amount of pee that they deposit whereas poo is often one big deposit. Pee can come in smaller, more frequent doses, as in the cases of marking or submissive and excitement uri-nation.

Time of appearance: Poo usually appears first thing in the morning and/or after food due to the way the digestive system works, so it is easier to predict when our puppy or dog will poo while training for complete housebreaking.

Release times: Poo requires more work and a longer release time. Sometimes our puppy can be a little pickier as to the location and/or the substrate of deposition. This is especially true if he has been previously disturbed or frightened during release. For this reason, some puppies may also require peace, quiet and privacy and may choose more hidden areas or may refuse to use a training pad to poo on.

Use: Poo is not used to mark territory as much as pee is.

Please note:

1. Wherever the author writes in first-person narrative it is Marilyn Peters, who is referring to herself (unless otherwise stated within the text).

2. As a matter of ease, we have referred to our problematic canine pee'er or poo'er as Pup (Puppy) or Dog depending on his/her age. We have made our toilet-troubled canine friend a male, without this meaning that males are in any way more prone to such behavioural issues. I think, also, we were influenced by Campari, whom you will meet a little later on, and who arrived just as we were in the middle of this book, and motivated us during it.

Introduction

by Klea Morianou

Writing a book just on dog toilet troubles sounds a bit extreme, right? When we proudly announced our project to friends and family, they gave us a rather condescending stare: *"What the heck? Why would these two girls want to spend so much time on such a project? They can surely do much better than that..."* one being a biologist, experienced animal behaviourist and author, and the second an architect, social scientist, animal welfare activist, journalist and TV producer.

A book that specializes in dog peeing and pooing sounds ludicrous to those who have never faced a confused home-soiling pooch. But we knew better, as we had both experienced hundreds of failed human-dog relationships purely because of dog toilet trouble. Dogs are unfortunately regularly abandoned because of soiling problems. Rescue dogs face a lifetime in shelters because of incomplete housebreaking issues, and puppy futures are 'destroyed' because of common mistakes and widespread misconceptions about toilet upbringing.

Toilet trouble is the number one challenge faced by Greek dog guardians, more serious even than separation anxiety, socialization, or even aggression. It is the most common reason for returning or even abandoning a dog. We both agreed that this had to stop.

Having acquired so much experience from all the toilet-trouble cases that we had been asked to assist with, we decided it would be a pity to let so much knowledge on the subject go to waste! I had successfully housed and toilet-trained dozens of rescue puppies and dogs (even old, blind and deaf ones) in my own home, and we had both offered counselling to hundreds of prospective rescue-dog and first-time puppy guardians. Marilyn would be called upon to deal with the most serious of our cases. Our toilet-related web articles were of the most popular amongst our readers.

Soon after our soiling initiative was announced, and this book's first chapters had been drafted, I was to face one big challenge. I had just welcomed an eight-week-old male golden retriever puppy into my family.

The puppy was considered potty-trained as he had learned to pee on training pads. So it should have been relatively easy to take the next step, right? I was extremely confident with potty training, as I had done 'the impossible' by potty training Fix, a deaf and blind insecure nine-year-old male dog who had been marking 25-30 times per day in the house, and pooing another 10-15, in the beginning. But the new puppy, soon to be known as Campari, proved the greatest challenge of all. He made me question my experience and almost had me abandon the pee-book project altogether: No 'Dog Pee & Poo Specialist' should face such trouble in housetraining a young, clever, easy-going retriever pooch, right?

But the truth is, I had never before lived with a 30 TPD (times per day) peeing puppy (see paragraph 'The 30 TPD peeing puppy'), who also had a clear preference for training pads (only unused ones, however, which substantially raised the cost of going to the puppy loo). *Plus* he was also a double pee-er—or rather a triple one (see paragraph 'What is a 'double-pee-er'?')—*and* he did not give pee notifications when crated (he preferred to wet himself). And as if this wasn't enough, Campari also had a fair liking for dog faeces. All this in one—the ultimate toilet trouble challenge!

Campari, has since grown to be a stable outdoor toilet-goer with a nine-hour straight (and dry) night sleep at the age of five months. Not bad, right?

Thanks to Campari, and all the difficulties that his situation entailed, we made a few last minute key chapter additions to our book that some of you may find extremely useful. And I have proudly gained back my confidence as a 'Dog Pee & Poo Specialist'. Hopefully, by the end of this book, you will also join the 'Dog Pee & Poo Specialist' club!

CHAPTER 1

Indoors is not acceptable, right?

Canine soiling inside a human house is not something that is acceptable in the human world. Not even for a puppy, and even more so for an adult dog. We do not want them soiling our houses, full stop. And quite rightly so. Nobody wants to be mopping up excrement within their own home, or to end up with a stinky house that nobody wants to enter. As much as this is true, and very understandable, it is also important to remember that these are human expectations and they are somewhat unrealistic when applied to dogs. When living with dogs, soiling inside the house will, at some point, inevitably happen, whether we like it or not, and, especially during puppyhood, more often than not. This is something that we should be aware of and accept as part of canine companionship. Accepting this will relieve a lot of pressure from our puppy and a lot of heartache from us. It is also the first step in the rehabilitation of any canine problem behaviour.

House soiling, whether frequent or infrequent, and in any form—such as leakage, small deposits of urine or faeces, or sometimes larger amounts left either in front of us or while we are away—is a very common occurrence and is officially considered a behaviour problem. House soiling is reported in approximately 20% of pet dogs (Wells and Hepper, 2000) and quickly manages to degrade the human-animal bond. It is a common reason for pet relinquishment (Salman, *et al.*, 2000; New *et al.*, 2000) and is, therefore, imperative that it is swiftly addressed.

A little tip from us to you is to avoid getting trapped in your own human expectations. If shit happens (excuse the pun!) do not take it personally, definitely do not panic, but do try to see things from your dog's perspective, as more often than not, there is either a message trying to be conveyed or a negative underlying emotion present, such as stress or anxiety, that is fuelling the behaviour. Whatever the case may be, there *are* solutions, so take a breath and relax.

When living with dogs, soiling inside the house will, at some point, inevitably happen, whether we like it or not.

1.1 Anxiety: the root of all evil!

Throughout all of my years of investigation into the root causes of canine behavioural problems, one underlying emotional state pops up like a nightmare again and again, either as a preliminary cause or as an enhancing secondary one: *anxiety*. Things are no different in the soiling sector of behavioural problems.

This prevalence of negative states plagues the canine population to varying degrees due to the fundamental and indisputable fact that dogs are living in a world alien to their own. And one thing is for sure: there is no chance of change unless we realise this fact, accept it and live together with a daily awareness of it.

Due to the severity of this problem and in the hope of raising awareness, we decided to dedicate a whole chapter of this book to anxiety. If there is any hope of increasing the wellness of our dogs, something that I know we all want for them, then we must understand just how anxious our pooches have become under our care, and most of the time without us even knowing it.

House soiling is reported in approximately 20% of pet dogs and manages to degrade the human-animal bond. It is a common reason for pet relinquishment and is, therefore, imperative that it is swiftly addressed.

1.2 Brave new world

Dogs, whether we realise it or not, do not, biologically speaking, belong in our reality—the human world. Sure, they have been living with us for thousands of years (some say even 130,000 years (Vilà *et al.* 1997)) and as a consequence, new behaviours have evolved from their proximity and connection to us, but this time period is not long enough, evolutionarily speaking, to change their fundamental biological nature. They are dogs, not humans, no matter how much we have humanised them, and they have a specific canine blueprint, one that they still share with their ancestors, the wild dogs, and so it is with them that their basic biological identity lies.

Even after their thousands of years next to us, dogs are still nothing but aliens in our world; strangers whose whole existence is completely controlled by humans; stripped of any inkling of choice whatsoever in all aspects of their daily life with us. We decide everything for them, including when they go out, where they go, what they eat, when they relieve themselves, where they relieve themselves, who they must be social with, etc. Additionally, they are expected by the human occupants of this world to instinctively know how to act and behave precisely and on command in all places and situations. They are expected to know how to communicate fully in a language that is not theirs, know where and how to go to the bathroom, know how to stay home alone, be social in all situations and with all kinds of human and animal energies and much much more. As Dr. Leslie Sinn rightly states in her excellent article "Is your Dog Perfect? No?": "Dogs are now expected to be a social extension of their guardians, not 'just a dog'". In other words, in most cases dogs are expected to be something they really are not. Our expectations are excessive, sometimes impossible to reach and, therefore, overpowering. This responsibility alone can be the cause of a lot of frustration and confusion that will eventually lead to anxiety.

Dogs are expected to know how to communicate fully in the language that is not theirs while suppressing their own means of communication.

1.3 Toilet-related confusion

So, let's focus on toilet related confusion and anxiety. As already mentioned, anxiety can be both a primary cause in soiling problems and/or a secondary one. This means that anxiety can appear *before* the first soiling incident, ie., pup soils as a result of anxiety, or it can appear *after* the soiling, usually due to the mishandling of the problem by the humans involved. In some cases, it can appear both *before* and *after* the soiling. Whether it appears before or after, it is certainly likely to continue to fuel the problem as a secondary influence if not recognised and dealt with. Either way, the anxiety has to be dealt with first and then the underlying cause of the anxiety must be addressed and eliminated.

Where does anxiety generally come from? How does it build up? The answer lies with confusion. That is how it all begins. So the next question is: how is confusion formed? Or how are we confusing our dogs when it comes to housebreaking?

Confusion can develop in a number of ways, but mainly when messages are not clearly and consistently projected to our dogs in a way that they can cognitively understand. Toilet training starts from day one and, therefore, so can confusion. Let's see how.

Where does anxiety generally come from? How does it build up? The answer lies with confusion. That is how it all begins.

Starting on the wrong foot

Whether a puppy or adult, the first behaviour that we are called upon to communicate to our dog when he first arrives is to pee and poo outside the house. Indoors is not acceptable for us humans. Our first ever expectation towards him, therefore, is:

"You must *not* pee or poo in the house."

Notice that this is a negative statement. Dogs do not understand the negative—they simply don't get it. In fact, by stressing the negative, we are more likely to enhance the negative behaviour because the dog will actually think that we are repeatedly showing him what we *do* want and not what we *don't* want. Dogs understand *only* the positive, so we would be much more successful if we made this expectation positive. The alternative positive statement would be:

"You must pee and poo outside."

If we started with projection of the more positive statement, communication would instantly be clearer and things would be easier and overall more positive for all involved. But we don't. We start our relationship with a negative expectation. A negative expectation immediately sets a negative energy and moves us in the direction of correction and punishment, rather than towards creating motivation with the aim of increasing the possibility of the positive outcome.

This is our first mistake. If we are not geared up and motivated to setting our dog up for success, then what we are actually doing is *waiting for him to make the mistake in order to correct*. Read 'Chapter 2: Why punishment is the wrong way to go' in order to understand what will come of punishment and correction and why you don't want to go down this path. *Punishment and correction creates confusion that later leads to anxiety.*

If we are not geared up and motivated to setting our dog up for success, then what we are actually doing is waiting for him to make the mistake in order to correct.

Creating a positive approach

A simple way of enhancing and communicating a positive expectation to your dog, as opposed to a negative one, is to physically show him repeatedly what it is you actually want from him. Take him outside at regular small intervals (see paragraph '4.5: The actual housebreaking process') to poo, and show him your pleasure by rewarding his effort and success with love and treats. Pleasing both you and himself will increase the possibility of it happening again the next time you go outside because, in fact, he really really *does* want to please you.

Summing up, what our puppy needs from us in order to cognitively understand our expectation regarding proper soiling behaviour is: love, patience, repetition, positive reinforcement and consistency.

A positive start, such as this, guarantees a happy, stress-free life with our dog, because its foundations will lie in mutual respect, love, trust, and clear communication. All these valuable assets are what will build that solid foolproof bond that is such a true blessing to experience.

1.4 The art of consistency

Consistency is a major theme throughout our lives with our dogs, and our lack of it is a common cause for canine confusion. As a consequence, it is also a serious cause of anxiety in our dogs.

Dogs thrive on consistency. Acting as a guideline in the human world, it gives them structure in their life and a way of predicting and knowing what is going to come next. We, on the other hand, are very rarely consistent with them. Even more so when communicating our toileting expectations. The good thing is that it is totally dependent on us whether they get consistency or not, and so, hopefully, if we are aware of the importance of consistency in their lives, we can step up. We can choose to be consistent or we can choose not to be (the former being the option of choice of course!). Whoever chooses not to be consistent should, in my opinion, not have a dog to begin with. Yes, it is *that* important for them in every aspect of their life with us.

Consistency must be applied to every part of their toilet training experience including:

- The location you want him to soil. It must not change.
- The time intervals between going outdoors. They should be the same.
- The times you take him out, i.e., after food, sleep etc., should be the same every day.
- Reinforcement. You must always reward until he learns.
- Cue words, e.g., *"Go peepee"*. They must not change.

Dogs thrive on consistency. Acting as a guideline in the human world, it gives them structure in their life and a way of predicting and knowing what is going to come next.

Dos and Don'ts: Avoiding potty associated anxiety

DOS

- Be patient
- Be consistent
- Use repetition
- Use positive reinforcement
- Be loving and compassionate
- Stay on a strict schedule
- If you catch him in the act, gently take him outside to finish the job
- Use enzymatic cleaners (see Chapter 2.3: The 'Correct Cleaning Protocol')
- Be prepared 'Exit Protocol' (see Chapter 4.7: The Exit Protocol)
- Be observant
- Learn the behavioural signs
- Use a crate or pen
- Remain relaxed

DON'TS

- Punish
- Shout
- Push his nose in the pee or poo
- Give him too much freedom
- Use training pads
- Be lazy
- Use different cue words
- Correct him after he has done it
- Make a fuss about cleaning it up
- Become obsessed with cleanliness
- Take accidents personally
- Become angry

1.5 Step nº1: Deal with the anxiety

Often and randomly (from the human perspective), anxiety shows its ugly face during a dog's life due to the difficulty associated with living with humans. It is, however, more likely to surface during times of change or after acute stress or trauma. Whether your puppy or dog has just arrived at your home, you have recently moved house, the family has grown—or reduced in size for that matter—or you already have a festering toilet problem on your hands, the probability that your dog is anxious is high. As long as anxiety is prevalent, there is no hope of teaching your puppy or dog proper housebreaking because processing any new information is limited in the presence of stress. Learning new behaviours, if there is already a pre-existing behavioural problem, is also restricted. In both cases anxiety leaves no room for change because the dog becomes completely blocked by it; rigid and stuck in a loop of desperation without the ability to see further than its own drama.

The number one step, therefore, in either a) preventing anxiety from taking over, or in b) breaking the vicious cycle of desperation when dealing with an actual toilet problem where anxiety is already high, is to first deal directly with the anxiety. Only then will the dog's brain be open to learning and therefore to change. There are a few natural remedies, such as rescue remedy, lavender, frankincense and neroli essential oils, that will help.

1.6 To summarise

Anxiety creates a fuzzy picture. It is difficult to see past it in order to help an animal displaying behavioural problems whether toilet related or otherwise. Soiling in the house, however, is, in my experience, quite often a symptom of some sort of underlying anxiety resulting usually from the confusion that we humans have created in our attempt to communicate with our dogs. Communication is an ongoing daily activity between human and dog and, if done incorrectly, creates confusion leading simultaneously to a constant level of ever-increasing daily stress and anxiety for our dogs. This anxiety may manifest in several very bizarre ways. It is necessary, therefore, to clear the fuzz away in order to get to the underlying predominant issue.

Soiling in the house is, quite often, a symptom of some sort of underlying anxiety resulting usually from the confusion that we humans have created in our attempt to communicate with our dogs.

CHAPTER 2

Why punishment is the wrong way to go

For us humans, a rather alarming yet true fact is that punishment is the easiest method of training for us to revert to. We do it all the time in our own lives, with our children and with each other. One could say that it comes to us almost naturally. Well, dogs are here to teach us otherwise because with them, and quite rightly, it simply *does not work*. Not only doesn't it work, but it will make matters much more complicated, and worsen any unwanted behaviour, even leading to aggression in the years to come. Catherine Taylor (2010) from Tulane University reports that three-year-old children that were spanked more frequently were much more likely to be aggressive by age five. Stanley Coren, Professor Emeritus in the department of Psychology at the University of British Columbia, shows in his research that dogs have the mental capacity approximating that of humans between two and three years of age. So why should punishment work any differently for dogs? Herron *et al.* (2009) conclude that animals that were trained using punishment are more likely to be aggressive. I have seen it time and again in my own work and it is always with great pain that I witness such an animal. Punishment creates nothing more than a broken animal and nasty, sometimes unresolvable rifts in our relationship with our dog.

As far as dogs are concerned, there are many positive ways to enhance and shape the desired soiling behaviour, or any behaviour for that matter. These ways involve proper communication through strong and loving connections with the animal, ways that allow the dog to cognitively understand exactly what is being asked of it and not be forced to comply through fear and correction. Although there are many ways of teaching positively, mainly through positive reinforcement, there is *one* sure-fire way to severely screw it up, and this way involves punishment. Punishment, in the way that humans usually do it, always ends in confusion and fear that later become anxiety and insecurity on many levels.

In this book, we offer proper behavioural techniques as well as some tips and tricks of our own to help speed up the puppy toilet training or dog toilet-related rehabilitative process. Be assured that if you don't use punishment there is only one way to go, and that way is forwards. Your puppy or dog will soon successfully be completely housebroken because dogs, by default, are clean animals and do not like to soil their home. But let's take things from the start.

"When I am peeing and pooing in the house, my people follow me around creating loud noises and making it all the more exciting, whereas when I am calm nobody pays any attention to me."

2.1 The answer to punishment

When Pup first comes home, and for the next few months, the plain truth is that he is likely to get himself into all sorts of trouble in his adventures around the house. He will be exploring the world with his teeth, as young animals with no hands tend to do, and will be peeing and pooing everywhere until he is completely housebroken. If punishment is our chosen method of teaching, we will have to scold Pup whenever he is doing something 'naughty' or has peed or pooed somewhere; that would mean scolding non-stop for most of the day. For the better part of each day, therefore, we will be turning our energy towards him while he is engaging in unwanted behaviour by shouting *"No!"* or *"You naughty boy! What have you done again?"* In contrast with our own previous behaviour, when Puppy is calm and sleeping we will find ourselves thanking the Lord while tip-toeing around the house making sure not to wake him lest the mischievous puppy awaken and start all over again. In hindsight, you can see that what is actually happening with this behaviour management scenario is that we are putting emphasis on 'bad' behaviour and ignoring good behaviour. Puppy learns that *"when I am chewing things or peeing and pooing in the house, my people follow me around creating loud noises and making it all the more exciting, whereas when I am calm nobody pays any attention to me"*. It is actually the opposite that we want.

The general rule for disciplining a puppy, therefore, is: REWARD what we want repeated i.e., calm behaviour, and IGNORE what we don't want repeated whenever possible. Whenever not possible, the secret is to DISTRACT.

To summarise, the misplacement of our attention via punishment may result in an increase in unwanted behaviours, such as persistent peeing or pooing in the house. These can quickly become very annoying—and sometimes dangerous—attention-seeking mechanisms. The saddest consequence of punishment, though, is the big wedge that is driven between guardian and Pup even before a solid relationship has had the chance to form. Pup becomes both confused and fearful and later anxious and insecure within his own home. The overall long-term result is an unbridgeable gap that will prohibit clear communication and encourage the onset of a variety of anxiety-related behavioural issues.

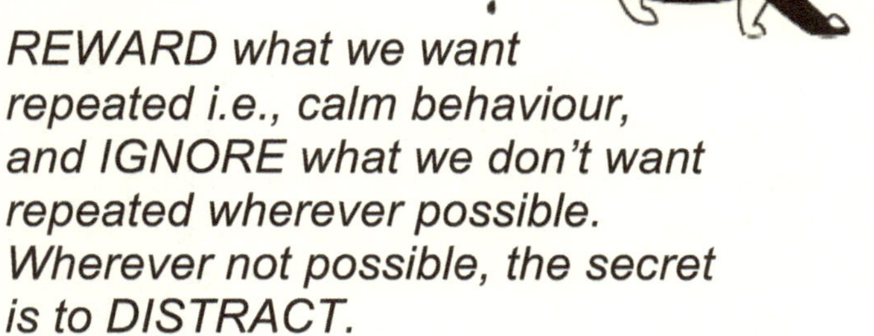

REWARD what we want repeated i.e., calm behaviour, and IGNORE what we don't want repeated wherever possible. Wherever not possible, the secret is to DISTRACT.

2.2 How to act when dog is caught in the act

One of the first and most common questions I get when consulting on how to deal with a persistent pee-er or pooer, is *"Okay, but what do we do to correct the behaviour if we see the dog doing it?"* When asked this question, I immediately know that the dog's carer is anxious about correcting his dog. The carer feels like there is something more proactive that should be done to make sure it doesn't happen again. Scolding is the first thing that comes to mind. As already mentioned, the answer is *not punishment*. Before answering questions, I usually take the time to emphasise how important it is to remain calm at all times and to put more energy into prevention rather than correction. All tips and advice found in this book aim at increasing the chances of you not having to find yourself in this position. If, however, you do catch Pup or Dog in the act, which is bound to happen at some point, then there is definitely a right and a wrong way of handling it. The wrong way is to become upset or disappointed and to run panic-stricken and screaming towards him in an attempt to stop him. The correct way is to remain calm and follow the following guidelines:

- ▶ ***Do not*** shout or scream or chase: we do not want to generate fear or he may start hiding from you in order to relieve himself.
- ▶ Go up to him, calmly yet swiftly, and either pick him up or hold him by the harness and take him outside. On the way you can still use your voice and the chin tickle mentioned in the 'Upright Leash Technique', (Chapter 6) to create a distraction.
- ▶ If he is on a leash (read the 'Umbilical Cord' technique in paragraph 6.2), say 'No!' and depending on his size either pick him up or walk him briskly to the outdoor soiling area using one finger to provide a

very slight upward tension on the line in order to maintain his attention.

▶ If walking, keep a good momentum and talk to him all the way in order to keep focus on you and distract him from his urge. For a more detailed description of this procedure please refer to paragraph 4.6: Upright leash technique.

▶ Wait with him outside until he has finished and reward him with a treat. You can even play a little after elimination.

▶ Bring him back inside.

▶ Clean up (in private) any mess that you didn't manage to prevent from happening, to avoid further accidents.

2.3 Proper cleaning of puddles and piles!

How you clean the area of an accident plays an important role in whether or not Pup will be encouraged to reuse the specific area again in the future. You see, urine is composed of three different substances; urea, urochrome (the yellow colour), and uric acid (Shojai; 2018). Urea and urochrome can be washed away, but uric acid is almost impossible to remove from surfaces and is the substance that Pup might be stimulated by (leading to reuse of the area) while walking past it in the future. It is recommended therefore not to use common household cleaners no matter how strong they are, but to purchase enzymatic cleaners specific for dealing with pet stains.

Do Not…

▶ Use ammonia-based cleaning products. The ammonia in the product will only serve to mimic the urine (since urine has ammonia in it) thereby converting your whole house into a big attractive toilet!

▶ Use bleach of any kind. Urine contains ammonia that when in contact with bleach results in the production of chloramine gas, which can cause coughing, shortness of breath, wheezing, nausea, watery eyes, irritation to the throat, nose and eyes, and pneumonia according to the Washington State Department of Health.

How you clean the area of an accident plays an important role in whether or not Pup will be encouraged to reuse the specific area again in the future.

What to do: The 'Correct Cleaning Protocol'

1. Start by picking up any solids and blotting dry as much of the liquid as possible with absorbent kitchen paper. Do not rub the area in an attempt to clean it because you will only succeed in creating a larger surface area that requires cleaning.
2. If cleaning upholstery or carpet:
   a. Soak the area with an apple cider vinegar: water mixture (1:1)
   b. Using a brush rub the area thoroughly. The vinegar will neutralise the ammonia.
   c. Let sit for a few minutes then wipe away with a wet cloth.
   d. Sprinkle some baking soda on the area
   e. Let sit for approximately two hours or, better still, overnight.
   f. Vacuum away the baking soda
   g. Clean with an enzymatic cleaner thoroughly.
3. If cleaning hard floors of any kind, the protocol is much simpler. After you have picked up the mess and dried the area you can move straight onto the application of the enzymatic cleaner. Follow the relevant instructions of the manufacturer for your specific product.
4. If you suspect that some accidents have gone unnoticed, you can always check by scanning the house with a black light. If you discover any surprises, the above guidelines will serve you well. However, more effort and several repetitions of the whole protocol may be required to remove the persistent stains.
5. You don't need an audience while cleaning! Please make sure that Pup or Dog is not watching your cleaning frenzy. Put him in another room and give him an interactive toy to keep him busy. We don't want to trigger any attention seeking patterns by associating the presence of his mess with your attention to him.

CHAPTER 3

Puppies and prevention

Proper prevention during puppyhood cannot be emphasised enough. It is well worth the trouble because it will ensure a calm and trouble-free adulthood, reducing to a minimum the heartache of having to tackle a full-blown behavioural problem somewhere down the road.

Proper prevention begins even before you hold Pup in your arms for the very first time. It starts with proper choice of puppy and ends with complete housebreaking: a time continuum that may last six months to a year. It has been shown that with appropriate preventive counselling, most puppy and new dog guardians are able to properly housetrain their dogs within one to two months of adoption (Herron *et al.,* 2007). In my opinion, however, this is a little over-optimistic as experience has shown me that it will, most probably, take longer. At the end of the day, it really depends on the dog and generalisations often prove short lived. A more realistic scenario, due to unexpected troubleshooting during this process, is between two to six months, but, more often than not, the six-month age mark seems to prevail. Two to six months may seem like a long time to you now, but it is nothing compared to the next 15 years (at least) that you have ahead of you with your dog. You will not regret the time, effort and energy you invested in your Pup at this very crucial stage of your life together. So, patience is definitely a virtue that you will have to call upon until Pup is soiling appropriately outside. Let's get down to the details of prevention.

3.1 Why is choosing a puppy SO important?

The decisions that you must make during the selection stage are responsible for determining your whole experience as a dog guardian, rendering it *the* most important stage in your life with your dog. We cannot emphasize this enough. Obvious first questions of this phase, but nonetheless, of paramount importance, are *"**Where** do I get my puppy from?"* and *"**When** do I get it?"* Puppy must not leave mum sooner that eight weeks of age and no later than 10 weeks. This is the optimum time for him to leave, as he is not yet overly dependent on his family and first environment, and has absorbed all vital lessons from mum and siblings that will help him become a balanced law-abiding adult.

The conditions that Puppy has been living in prior to his arrival at your home, i.e., in the first two months of life, greatly affect many aspects of Pup's adult life. Toilet trainability and how 'clean' he will generally be within your home are also aspects affected by these relevant living conditions. These conditions will be imprinted and carried along with him as preferences.

It is during the ninth week of development (eight and a half weeks old), within the window of socialisation, that dogs conclude on their preference for a toilet substrate (Overall, 1997). What this means is that whatever he was soiling on before and during this time may become his preferred future substrate.

The infamous 'window of socialisation', the most sensitive time in his life, begins at the age of three weeks and ends at 16 weeks of age. The time spent with his breeder, or anywhere for that matter, before meeting you, falls into this sensitive window where Pup is most open to external influence from his environment. Therefore habits, good or bad, will have formed before you even meet him.

Later on in life, as an adult, Pup will be challenged with varying stimuli such as hormone changes, life changes (moving house, new flatmate, change in routine) and fear factors (how fearful he will become will depend on the level of his socialisation). A healthy start in life, in other words a 'clean' start in life, combined with a good socialisation programme, will better equip Pup to be more adaptable to any changes that he encounters and not start soiling uncontrollably in your house with the first encounter of stress.

It is during the ninth week of development, within the window of socialisation, that dogs conclude on their preference for a toilet substrate.

3.2 From where?

If your puppy has been kept at the breeder's or in a pet shop in a small puppy pen, as is commonly done, with newspapers or pads as substrates, and has been allowed to soil repeatedly in this area, he will have learned that *"we soil in our space"*, which goes against dogs' natural instinct. Without frequent cleaning and in, therefore, dirty conditions, Puppy will learn that this is the norm and when entering your home he will bring these dirty bad habits with him. It will take longer to teach him that his crate or pen is not a toilet, and he may even eat his faeces either as a game or in an attempt to clean his area. The consumption of faeces is a behaviour called coprophagia (see Chapter 8: Coprophagia: a disgusting habit for some).

In addition, if during his short life before you, non-absorbent substrates were used—such as newspapers that drip and become soggy or slip and shift around bunching up in corners of the pen as Pup moves—excrement will have undoubtedly ended up on the floor or Puppy will have soiled the floor instead of the newspapers. The presence of pee on the floor or soiling the floor will lead to a preference for floors in your puppy's mind. The same applies if Pup, for other reasons, has already had access to floors over a period of time and has consistently soiled them. Unfortunately, this means that he will arrive in your life already programmed to soil floors. The type of floors that Pup builds a preference for will depend solely on the type of floor he was soiling on as a puppy. This includes all types of hard floors and also carpeted ones. A preference for floors means that, if not reprogrammed as soon and as vigilantly as possible, then later on in life, and as a result of any form of stressor, Dog may easily go back to relieving himself on the floor, especially if this act results in stress relief for him.

Bad habits, picked up from the breeders or elsewhere, require extra time and energy to reverse. Fortunately, at this age, Pup's little mind is highly flexible and as long as you have prior knowledge regarding his history and are persistent in your future guidance, you should not have any further problems. There must, however, be no opportunity given to Puppy for soiling any place other than your designated soiling area.

Buying animals from a pet shop is not a good idea. It usually means, for the most part, a number of serious behavioural and medical conditions later on in your animal's life.

Pet shop trouble

Buying animals from a pet shop is not a good idea. It usually means, for the most part, a number of serious behavioural and medical conditions later on in your animal's life. Pet shops usually source their animals from large breeding units i.e., production mills, where conditions are often subpar and sometimes outright horrendous. The animals are treated and handled as commodities, roughly and without respect. They are usually separated from Mom too early, and have incurred long, stressful and uncomfortable travel before arriving to the pet shop. Consequently, this most sensitive period in their lives, when they are still so small and vulnerable, and where everything registers, is dominated by stress and fear. We therefore do not recommend that you look to pet shops for your animal companion. Rather, we advise that you find a small-scale breeder who mimics the conditions of your own home and who has spent time and energy socialising his/her puppies. We want Pup to experience as carefree and stress-free a transition from breeder to forever home as possible at this tender age. This choice alone will greatly reduce the possibility of Pup growing up into an insecure, fearful and sick animal.

We want our puppy to experience as carefree and stress-free a transition from breeder to forever home as possible at this tender age.

Rescue puppies

Rescue puppies are a whole different ball game. Unfortunately, their histories vary from individual to individual making it very hard for us to generalise about soiling issues. However, they will usually fall into one of two categories. Those, and unfortunately this is the majority, that have had a fearful and traumatic start to life on the streets or in shelters, and those that haven't, i.e., have been born in more sheltered conditions with care from the public and more exposure to people. Most rescue puppies have, however, at some point, experienced little to no exposure to humans, and unfortunately, if they have, it usually is of a negative nature. Fear and stress prevail during their socialisation period, from their time on the streets or in shelters, and so it is completely dependent on their character as to how and if these scars will surface, and to what extent it will affect them as adults.

Street life or shelter life means that Pup has already been peeing and pooing in an outdoor environment, usually earth or concrete slabs, and has therefore, purely by chance, formed a preference for the outdoors at the proper age of eight weeks, as opposed to purebred puppies that have known only the indoors. Hence, rescue puppies are often 'cleaner' than purebred puppies and readily eliminate outdoors without much effort on our part. Having that initial preference for the outdoors is an advantage and should be acted upon, as it will mean that Rescue Pup will also initially hold his sphincter muscles—as much as he can according to his age—until he is given access to the outdoors. So long as you are tuned in and give him outdoor access quickly when he feels the urge, you will easily avoid the initial accidents that are so common at the beginning of toilet training.

These are the pros of a rescue puppy as far as toilet etiquette goes. There are also cons. The cons you encounter depend solely on the character of your puppy and his early life experiences. Where Pup chooses to eliminate will depend on where he has spent the most time eliminating before he met you, just as any breeder puppy. If he has been eliminating on concrete, the flooring of choice for most shelters, then this is what he will seek out, and he will find it difficult to eliminate on earth to begin with.

Additionally, although initially the preference for the outdoors is there, his bladder and anal sphincter muscles are virtually untrained in holding any urine or faeces as he has peed and pooed for the most part whenever he felt the urge to, and most probably within his kennel space at the shelter, thereby learning, against canine instincts, that it is okay to soil his home. This means that bad habits may have again formed and it is in your hands, with the help of a good training programme, to reprogramme your pup as he has had no restrictions or reason for holding himself before entering your human family.

Housebreaking, in itself, is an unnatural human expectation for a dog. In nature, feral dogs relieve themselves wherever and whenever they like, with the only exception being their immediate sleeping quarters.

If rescue Pup is especially fearful, initial housebreaking will be more challenging. He might be afraid of the outdoors for whatever reason—noises, lights, cars, traffic, people etc.—and this fear may make him freeze outside. If this is the case, he may need an indoor soiling area, preferably next to, or close to the front door until he feels more comfortable in his surroundings. In this case we suggest a large box full of earth as a toilet as opposed to train-ing pads (see paragraph '4.3 Puppy training pads: A short term light relief').

When adopting a rescue puppy, first priority must be to make Pup feel safe and secure and trusting in us. He needs a quiet and stable environment with a predictable daily routine. Toilet training is the same for Rescue Pup as for any other puppy. However, due to possible extenuating circumstances in his life, empha-sis must be given on handling the puppy in a very gen-tle, respectful and relaxed way, so as not to cause more pressure on the already overwhelmed puppy; to be frank, this is something we believe all puppies de-serve, coming into our home, regardless of their place of origin.

It is only in the human world that dogs must master the art of soiling wherever and whenever their human wants them to, as opposed to when they actually physically need to.

Just like it is not expected of a child to be born with the knowledge that he/she must go to a certain room of the house and use the toilet in a specific way, the same applies to a dog.

3.3 Ready, steady, go!

Whether acquired from a breeder, a shelter or rescued from the streets, the fact is that your new housemate is still a puppy. So, accidents are bound and expected to happen, both before and during housebreaking training. Just like it is not expected of a child to be born with the knowledge that he/she must go to a certain room of the house and use the toilet in a specific way, the same applies to a dog. This knowledge must be learned; moreover, it must be learned in a specific way and at a specific time, when the individual is both physically and psychologically ready to absorb and use it.

Housebreaking, in itself, is an unnatural human expectation for a dog. In nature, feral dogs do not need to learn to control their sphincter muscles because they relieve themselves wherever and whenever they like, with the only exception being their immediate sleeping quarters. In fact, frequent depositions of urine and faeces are often required in order to mark their territory. It is only in the human world, therefore, and as a result of domestication, that they must master the art of soiling wherever and whenever their human wants them to, as opposed to when they actually physically need to. Since it is our expectation, one of many, it is also our responsibility to teach them this strange new behaviour in a way that they will understand. It is also our duty to show understanding, patience, respect and tolerance during this process.

Since it is our expectation, one of many, it is also our responsibility to teach them this strange new behaviour in a way that they will understand. It is also our duty to show understanding, patience, respect and tolerance during this process.

CHAPTER 4
Complete housebreaking for puppies and adult dogs

4.1 There is no magic way!

There is only one proper method for complete housebreaking that will guarantee long term results, whether you are training a puppy for the first time or are rehabilitating an adult soiler. Unfortunately there is no magic formula involved. This method has no fixed variables and requires, from the human, large amounts of repetition, patience and persistence until the dog's brain has become programmed to human standards and all accidents have ceased for at least three months. Only then can one conclude that the dog has been completely housebroken. Additionally, there is also no standard time frame to refer to regarding the length of time that this process should take, or the age at which the dog should be completely housebroken. Every dog is different. Some dogs will pick up on the new information quickly and may only take a few days to set a predictable toilet schedule, others may take months. Just keep at it.

Before delving into the actual proposed training or rehabilitation housebreaking method, let's clarify some points by looking at important facts regarding common

housebreaking tools, such as crates and training pads. Let's also discuss vaccinations and their place during housebreaking, and revisit why punishment is absolutely the wrong way to go.

Proper use of the crate requires that Pup remains inside only a) during the night and b) for short periods during the day when it is not possible to watch him.

4.2 Crates, pens and spatial restriction

Spatial restriction in the form of a crate or pen is recommended as a very handy tool for the beginning. Not only is it practical, but it is also something that Pup and Dog can readily relate to. A small, confined, yet comfortable and fun-filled space mimics the litter's natural den. Pups spend most of their day within the safe environment of their den playing, eating and sleeping, but they do not soil inside. Therefore, a den within your home will help Pup or Dog (if re-training an adult dog) start holding themselves as they instinctively will not want to soil the den. The idea is that if Pup is given free range of the whole house, or access to a big open space within, it will be more difficult and frustrating to keep a constant eye on him. Unsupervised roaming in the house will a) make accidents much more probable, b) increase the likelihood of Pup slipping away unnoticed up the stairs or to some other secluded spot to relieve himself, and c) result in a very tired, frustrated and flustered human.

Although a crate or pen can be a handy tool, it can become negative for Pup or Dog if not used properly. In the wild, puppies have free access to the outdoors as their den is not locked and so they do not need to hold themselves for long before they can find relief. It may only be a matter of seconds to begin with. The same must occur with the crate or pen. As already mentioned, the aim is to provide a safe and comfortable restricted environment and not a prison. If its use is abused and Pup remains inside for too long every day, isolated from his environment, then not only will it lose its use as a housebreaking tool—because it will get soiled and Pup will get used to soiling it—but it will also start creating stress and social isolation that, if experienced at this age, will be detrimental to his development. Proper use requires that Pup remains inside only a) during the night and b) for short periods during the day, when it is not possible to watch over him. Examples of such times could be when you are at work, when you must pop out to run errands, or when you are momentarily busy within the home and not able to observe him—e.g., housecleaning, talking on the phone or having a shower. The more Pup is free but under observation, the more he can integrate with the family and the quicker he can become a member with full appreciation for rules and boundaries. It is therefore imperative that the majority of the day Pup is out of his crate and mingling with us and the rest of the family.

Although a crate or pen can be a handy tool, it can become negative for Pup or Dog if not used properly.

4.3 Puppy training pads

A short-term light relief...

Puppy training pads, despite their expense, are very often used during housebreaking to indicate to Pup an acceptable soiling area within the home. They are used as a compromise solution between the indoors and the outdoors, purely for practical reasons. Using them makes it easier to prevent accidents (and excessive mopping!) and does not require much effort on our part, because when there is a pad close by, Pup does not have to be taken all the way outside. However, there are also cons to consider when using training pads, as they may trigger bigger problems in the long run.

... a long-term pain in the butt!

Personally, I do not like to use them. Not only are they (and newspapers) a serious health hazard for a puppy due to the very real possibility of ingestion during bouts of play resulting in vomiting and intestinal blockages, they are also the initial cause for many other behavioural and welfare problems that may emerge. Therefore, I never recommend them.

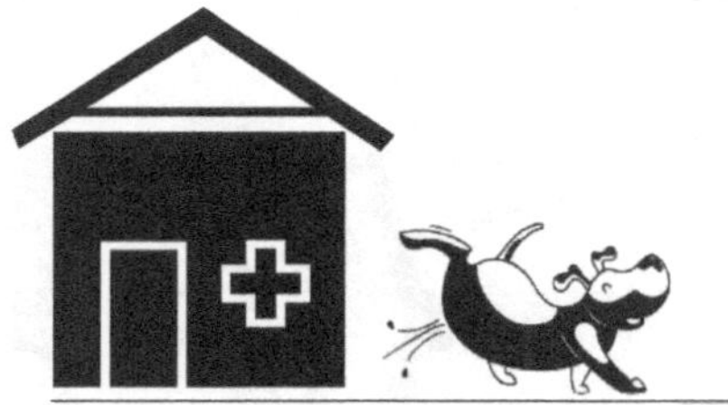

Training pads can be a serious health hazard for a puppy due to the very real possibility of ingestion during bouts of play resulting in vomiting and intestinal blockages.

Using pads adds more learning steps to the whole housebreaking programme for the already overwhelmed puppy.

My main objection against using training pads or newspapers, even as a temporary solution for a short length of time, is that by using them Pup gets used to soiling inside the house, even if it is just in one spot. It becomes okay in his canine mind; a possibility, something that can be done. I don't want this possibility to ever exist within a dog's mind. It should never ever cross his mind, not at any life stage or age, that soiling within the house is anywhere close to a possibility. This possibility simply should not exist, just like soiling his own den in the wild does not exist. Creating such a possibility within Pup's mind increases the chance that later on in life, as a result of stress or hormonal changes, Dog may easily resort to soiling the house again, in order to relieve himself. This behaviour can then easily become a pattern and soon Dog will be urinating or defecating in other areas of your home as well. This is a scenario that I have very often encountered, and it is always interesting to see that favourite soiling areas usually include ones that resemble pads in some way, such as small carpets, bathroom mats, or other cloth-type mats or areas. If however, from a pup, he *never* learned to soil in the house, not even in a designated area, then it will be almost impossible for him to form a habit should a soiling accident occur later on in adult life, simply because the option to pee in the house never existed to begin with.

Using pads unfortunately has more disadvantages. One of these is that, for the already overwhelmed puppy, it adds more learning steps to the whole house-breaking programme. Rather than creating one easy learning step in his mind such as:

1. 'Learn to pee and poo outside,'

we add *two* extra unnecessary learning steps, complicating things for no reason. The learning steps now look like this:

1. 'Learn to pee and poo on the pad in the house.'
2. 'Learn to pee and poo outside.'
3. 'Forget the pad.'

During each transition between learning steps, Pup is expected to not only learn something new, but also forget previous learnt behaviours. Meanwhile, to make things worse, people frequently also find it appropriate to begin punishing Pup for previously learned steps (i.e., soiling the pad, or the area where the pad used to be—behaviours which he was previously consistently rewarded for) while teaching the new learning step. This causes great confusion and subsequent stress for the puppy.

Convenience, combined with the misconception that small dogs do not need exercise, ensure that Dog ends up confined to the house and deprived entirely of his walks.

A major welfare issue

As if this all wasn't enough, there is also a major welfare issue associated with the use of training pads and that is the significant delay caused in Pup experiencing the outdoors. People get comfortable with the convenience offered by the training pads and, as a result, continue to use them for longer than needed—sometimes even for life. Small breed dogs in particular suffer mostly from this. Convenience, combined with the misconception that small dogs do not need exercise, ensure that Dog ends up confined to the house and deprived entirely of his walks. Such imprisonment has severe consequences in the long run, as the walk is Dog's most vital of all biological canine needs. Depriving him of walks leads to a miserable life of incarceration, lack of stimulation, hyperactivity, lack of socialization and general madness. Additionally, it will create heightened insecurity in the human world, increasing the possibility of severe fears and phobias appearing. It is the equivalent of locking a human within the confines of one room for years, something that will surely drive him crazy. House arrest, therefore, quickly becomes a serious welfare issue for any dog.

Even if incarceration doesn't happen though, most pups, in my experience, do end up reaching three to four and even five months of age without ever having soiled outdoors. This is way too long! The unavoidable result is a puppy that happily relieves himself indoors, and less happily outside. Indoors becomes a place that offers more security, seeing that it is more familiar, quiet, and infused with known scents, whereas outdoors gets associated with the unknown; this huge antithesis can create insecurity, fear and a sense of danger. The longer Pup soils indoors, the harder it becomes to change his ways and to train him to soil outside. Some dogs never learn to go outdoors and are, as a result, stripped of the opportunity of engaging in very instinctive and beneficial behaviours, such as exchanging information with their four-legged neighbors by means of marking.

Neighborhood dogs are constantly processing the information left by other individuals while on their walk, and consequently answering by creating their own scent trail. This leads to a conversation between them by means of scent alone, via the exchange of information-packed urine and faecal deposits. Believe it or not, any instinctive behaviour, such as marking, is beneficial for your dog as it provides important and much-needed mental stimulation for them during their day. Should he be allowed to do it, it will serve to increase his welfare substantially. Scent communication is not well understood by humans yet, but it is a large part of canine communication; some say even more so than visual communication via body language.

Toilet training, which is part of socialisation, and socialisation itself, both require Pup to be exposed to the outdoors as much as possible. Vaccination protocols, however, require the opposite.

There has to be a middle ground somewhere where puppies are kept safe from disease, but are given the best opportunity to gain all the benefits that come with early exposure to the outdoors.

A necessary evil or is there another solution?

If one must, for whatever reason, use an indoor toilet, rather than pads, which create a very artificial and far from natural experience for the Dog, I prefer that it be one that resembles, as much as possible, more what a proper natural doggy toilet should be, i.e., it should resemble the outdoors. This means that it should smell and feel like the outdoors. Such a toilet can easily be created using a large plastic basin for puppies and small breed dogs, or a handcrafted wooden base lined with large plastic garden sheets for a larger animal. The substrate of preference should be nothing other than soil that you can find either straight from a garden or from a nursery. The toilet should be situated either in an outdoor part of the house, for example a balcony or terrace, or, if this isn't possible, next to or near the front door. This way, when the transition from indoors to outdoors is made, it can be done so in a much easier and stress-free manner.

Whatever you choose to use as an indoor toilet, i.e., training pads or litter box, its use should be faded out very quickly, i.e., as soon as Pup has started using it regularly!

4.4 Toilet training and vaccinations

Toilet training, socialisation and vaccination protocols clash. This is the plain truth. They all occur during the socialisation period and are contradictory by nature. Toilet training, which is part of socialisation, and socialisation itself, both require Pup to be exposed to the outdoors as much as possible in order to ensure that he a) learns to soil properly outside the house and b) becomes a balanced, confident adult in the human world. Vaccination protocols, however, require the opposite, i.e., that he remain indoors until fully vaccinated in order to avoid contracting deadly diseases.

The inarguable need for good socialisation means that there has to be a middle ground somewhere where Pup is kept safe from disease, but is given the best opportunity to gain all the benefits that come with early exposure to the outdoors, as there are many and they are too important to be ignored. Dr. Kersti Seksel, in Veterinary Medicine's roundtable discussion on early puppy socialisation classes, explains that "the risk of being euthanized or surrendered (to a shelter) is much greater in unsocialized, untrained dogs than the risk of dying from infectious diseases" (AVSAB, 2009). It is therefore great that the veterinary community has, since 2008, officially recognised the importance of socialisation via the help of veterinary behaviourists.

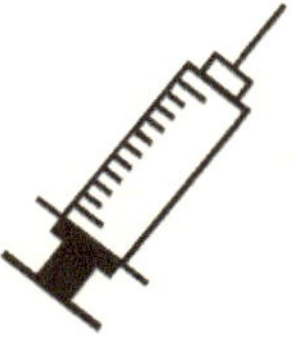

Toilet training, socialisation and vaccination protocols clash. This is the plain truth. They all occur during the socialisation period and are contradictory by nature.

In 2008, the American Veterinary Society of Animal Behavior released a position paper (AVSAB, 2008) outlining the importance of early puppy socialization, preferably *before* Pup reaches 12-16 weeks of age. The AVSAB encourages guardians to take their dogs to puppy classes as early as possible, even before they have completed their full vaccination series.

It is too easy to justify house confinement by masking it as 'protection of Pup', whereas the underlying emotion is merely one of outdated fears that prevent clear thinking. If overprotection is chosen, Pup will be approximately four to five months old by the time he sees the outdoors or goes to puppy classes for the first time, as opposed to around two months old (i.e., after the first vaccination has produced a measurable level of antibody immunity), when most puppy classes start today. By four months old, Pup will already be unsocial towards people and other dogs and animals, even if he isn't displaying fear behaviour yet. Fear behaviour will, however, latently arise between five to eight months of age where he will show fear responses and be less adaptable to all stimuli that the outdoors holds. Many lessons will have been lost and many bad habits acquired, exponentially increasing the possibility of serious behavioural problems in the future. With the help of some simple rules, however, a compromise can be met:

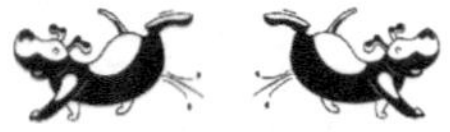

Simple rules for safe toilet training outdoors

1. Use your fenced garden for toilet training.
2. If you don't have a garden, choose a protected small outdoor piece of land outside or around your house that other animals do not visit or use as a toilet.
3. Every day, take Puppy out into the world in your hands or in a carrier, giving him the opportunity to observe the world without stepping on the road. If Puppy needs to go pee while outside, then either use another protected clean space, e.g., someone else's garden.
4. Arrange playdates with other vaccinated friendly dogs in their home or fenced garden.

Meanwhile you can help his socialization, while keeping him safe by:

5. Going to puppy classes.
6. Creating different new daily experiences within the home and/or the garden, for example by building obstacle courses using tunnels, climbing steps, sandpits, or different tactile surfaces that also make noise when stepped on.
7. Inviting other families (with children) to your house for play and socialisation.
8. Taking Puppy on car rides to new places.
9. Exposing him positively and calmly to all stimuli that he is likely to come across in his life in the human world, including gradually different means of transport (cars, buses, traffic, trains, underground/metro/subway), and different handling procedures (nail trimming, ear inspection, eye inspection, grooming).

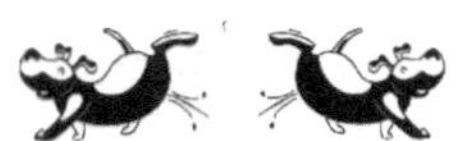

4.5 The actual housebreaking process

The ultimate goal during this process is to experience as few accidents as possible. Accidents will only serve to allow for indoor preferences regarding location and substrate to form (Dunbar, 2004), so the fewer the overall accidents, the easier it will be for Pup to understand that soiling is *only* allowed outside. To put it another way, the more Pup soils in the house, even if it is only by accident, the more ingrained it becomes in his little mind that soiling in the house is normal within the human reality.

Whether you have a garden or not, you should use prevention, rather than correction, as your mode of action.

The first few days

Housebreaking begins the moment Pup or Rescue Dog enters his new home. It is ideal, therefore, to have planned for his arrival beforehand and to have set aside a few days off work in order to set the best possible grounds for a clean fresh start with your new friend. You can either choose to bring him home during holidays or intentionally take time off of work.

If you have a garden, at this stage of housebreaking you are extremely privileged as it is much easier to just quickly open the door and let him out rather than pick him up and rush him down flights of stairs, or wait for a lift to arrive. Either way, it *has* to be done. If you don't have a garden then you must be extra vigilant and observant. In any case, you should use prevention, rather than correction, as your mode of action.

The first few days are to be expected to be days of misses, near misses and frustration until you and Pup settle down into some sort of routine. Know and accept this fact, relax about it, and then it will be easier. Do not give up. Be prepared for at least 10-12 small outings during the day. Vigilant observation is paramount. Good, clear organisation and planning will help you stay on top of things. Most importantly, make sure that before you start you have chosen a predesignated soiling area, preferably outside of the house, i.e., your garden, a small outdoor patch or an indoor toilet (e.g., a large box full of earth). This is where you will repeatedly be taking Pup to relieve himself during the first stages of toilet training.

Misses and near misses are to be expected in the beginning until you and Pup settle down into some sort of routine. Know and accept this fact, relax about it, and then it will be easier.

The morning

In order to increase your chances of quick success, start your peeing routine first thing in the morning upon opening your own eyes, or even before that(!), if you are lucky enough to have been notified by Pup when his urge arises. Either way, as soon as you wake up, and still in your pyjamas, without even relieving yourself first, pick Pup up gently and take him outside to the designated peeing and pooing area. Now you are ready to witness his first successful soiling of the day. To encourage him to be successful, you have to create the perfect opportunity by following a few simple steps that must strictly be repeated during each outing:

1. Wait quietly, while ignoring any motions made with the intent to engage you in play, until Pup has relieved himself.
2. You can add a cue like 'go potty' or 'go wee wee' by constantly repeating it while you are out. He will—with repetition—associate this cue with the act of peeing and pooing and quickly will be eliminating on cue.
3. Within seconds of relieving himself, and no later, Pup must get rewarded by receiving a treat and a small playtime (see below, 'Why play after each outdoor soiling session?'). This reward, in addition to the scent of his own urine, are what make Pup recognise, in his little brain, this specific area as a preferred soiling spot the next time he returns. As Overall (2011) states:

"A reward may help encourage the association between squatting on that substrate and good experiences. Urinating and defecating are physiologically self-rewarding; you are rewarding the behaviour exhibited in the location chosen".

In the morning, during this first outing from his den, he must ideally do both No1 and No2 before re-entering the house. If No2 doesn't happen within approximately 20 minutes, then bring him back inside and give him his first meal of the day. No2 will soon arrive—five or ten minutes after his first meal—so make sure to take him out again soon after. Well done! Now you have set yourself and Pup up for a successful day, having already achieved a clean morning. You can use your watch to help you schedule the rest of the day.

Within seconds of relieving himself, and no later, Pup must get rewarded by receiving a treat and a small playtime.

The rest of the day

When first starting out, as already mentioned, Puppy (or Rescue Dog) will pee and poo very often during the day. Again, the exact frequency differs between dogs. Some puppies will deposit small amounts of urine as frequently as every 20-30 minutes (see paragraph 'The 30 TPD peeing puppy'), and even sooner if excited during play; others will get the urge at larger intervals, such as every hour or so. The ultimate aim is to be prepared and to catch Pup each time *before* an accident happens. Until you get to know Pup and the frequency of his soiling bouts, however, it is best for the first few days to give ample access to the outdoors. I would say, to begin with, every 20-30 minutes is reasonable, especially for frequent soilers. Soon, however, he should be happy with an outing every hour to hour and a half. This time gap will become gradually larger and larger as he grows (see paragraph '4.9 Graduating to adult toilet savoir vivre').

To recap, from the first morning outing onwards and for the rest of the day, you must have your eye on the clock, and discreetly on Pup, and give regular access to an acceptable outdoor soiling area, in order to prevent any accidents within the home.

On the upside, there are certain times when it is more likely that Pup will want to go. These times are a) after food, b) after a nap, or c) during and after bouts of play. You will soon start to recognise and predict when Puppy needs to go because there will be indications in the form of behavioural cues that you will start to pick up on. These include suddenly moving away from the play area, intense sniffing of the ground, circling around himself, and lowering of the body. Some puppies also get a little agitated, especially before defecation, and engage in what we call 'the pee-poo dance'. Upon immediate observation of any of these behaviours, gently pick up your puppy without scaring or startling him and take him outside to the designated pee and poo area. Again, as already mentioned in the morning routine, wait with him patiently and quietly, reward him just as he finishes, and play a little afterwards.

The pee-poo dance steps

What behavioural cues show his need to soil?
- Suddenly moving away from the play area
- Intense sniffing of the ground
- Circling around himself, and lowering of the body
- Increase in excitement, agitation, possibly some barking

If you insist on using a training pad (which we do not recommend), you do, and your puppy misses the training pad by a little in his first few attempts, still reward his effort, then soak a small corner of the pad in the urine and leave it for the next time. In the beginning, but only until he catches on, it will help to always use some urine or another attractant (which you can find in any pet shop) on a small area of the training pad; by smelling it he will be stimulated to soil again in the same area. If Puppy is super clean, though, he may want a clean pad each time, but this preference usually becomes evident a little later on, once he has already learnt.

If Puppy keeps missing the training pad by a little, you can also try to increase the soiling area by laying more than one training pads next to each other and, after Puppy has mastered targeting the pad area, gradually decrease it.

When is it more likely that Pup will want to soil?

- After food
- After a nap
- During and after bouts of play

From the first morning outing onwards and for the rest of the day, you must have your eye on the clock, and discreetly on Pup, and give regular access to an acceptable outdoor soiling area.

Why play after each outdoor soiling session?

Providing a little playtime outside after soiling is an important step in toilet training. It is not only a fun reward that helps increase the chances that Pup will soil outside faster next time in anticipation of the game, but also it provides a little time lapse from the moment of release until returning indoors. This interval of time can serve three important purposes:

1. It can be used to avoid the association *"As soon as I pee, I go back inside"* from forming; an association that will cause an exuberant social puppy to delay going to the toilet next time because he may not want to go back inside because *"Outside is more fun!"*

2. It can help create a positive association with the outdoors, especially for timid puppies. This second purpose also highlights the importance of not being in a hurry and staying calm and positive whilst outdoors. Being in a negative state outside may create a negative association between Puppy and the outdoors, i.e., *"Whenever we are outside my human is angry and grumpy,"* which may lead to future refusal of venturing outside. So, take a big breath and learn to camouflage your frustration and impatience by whistling to yourself silently while he goes about his business.

3. It can help make the whole experience more positive for the human as well, thereby creating a stronger bond faster; *"Playing with Pup is always fun and worth the cold wait."*

The time lapse from the moment of release until returning indoors can help create a positive association with the outdoors, especially for timid puppies.

Providing a little playtime outside after soiling is a fun reward that helps increase the chances that Pup will soil outside faster next time in anticipation of the game.

During the night

Pup, when he first comes to you at two-to-three months of age, is the equivalent of a two-year-old child. Smaller-sized dogs generally mature faster than larger breeds, but whatever the case may be, you must keep reminding yourself that he is still only a very small baby—a baby that, usually, is not yet capable of holding itself throughout the night. Ideally, therefore, he will need access to the designated soiling area during the night also. This means that, initially, you will have to set your alarm clock approximately twice during the night. If done diligently, it will not be long before you can fade out your night-time outings as he will soon be able to hold himself throughout the night. Holding themselves throughout the night is the first thing that they learn regarding toilet training.

Once dry nights have been achieved, things become easier during the day too, with larger intervals between eliminations. In order to achieve a dry night, it is important that his last soiling session be as late as possible the previous night; ideally when all home activity has ceased, just before you yourself get to bed.

Holding himself throughout the night is the first thing that Pup needs to learn regarding toilet training. Once dry nights have been achieved, things become easier during the day too.

Night-time alarm settings

First week
Last pee and poo at midnight
1st alarm: 3am
2nd alarm: 6am
And then again at 8am or 9am as their first morning outing

Second week
Last pee and poo at midnight
1st alarm: 4am
And then again at 8am or 9am as their first morning outing

Third week
Last pee and poo at midnight
1st setting: 5am
And then again at 8am or 9am as their first morning outing

4.6 'Upright Leash' technique while travelling to the loo
By Klea Morianou

One of the most challenging parts of the puppy training period is the journey to the loo. We need to keep it dry all the way, until we reach the designated soiling area, which may prove a challenge if Pup or Dog is too big to carry in our arms, or if the trip to the loo is too long. For instance, if the journey includes long corridors, usage of the elevator, stairs, opening and closing doors, and Puppy has to walk to get to the loo, it is almost certain that he will leak. To avoid accidents along the way, we can try the 'Upright Leash' technique, but *only* for puppies and dogs that already know and are comfortable with the harness and leash. The 'Upright Leash' technique, combined with fast reflexes (as there is not a second to waste!) and an enthusiastic high-pitched voice, will increase the chances of Pup using his sphincter muscles to hold it all in during the journey to the loo.

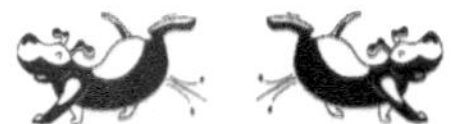

The 'Upright Leash' technique

For puppies and dogs that already know and are comfortable with the harness and leash

As soon as Pup sounds the first toilet alarm we need to be standing by the door with Pup tied to leash, keys in hand (or attached to a lanyard worn around the neck), and coat on if needed ASAP. In order to succeed:

1. Keep the leash in one hand, while using the other to give it a slight upward and forward tension. This creates a distraction for Pup, keeping his mind on the front end of his body rather than the back end. We suggest using a second hand because it helps keep just a slight amount of tension (without overdoing it).

2. Throughout the journey towards the loo, maintain a fast but steady pace and talk to Pup with enthusiasm in order to create a diversion. Make funny noises or talk silly for all that he cares. Do not, however, go over the top and get him too over-excited, as this will lead to him finding it harder to keep it all in. The whole point is to help him forget that he is in urgent need of peeing.

3. Enhance the effect of the 'Upright Leash' technique by using a small tickle under his chin, while moving towards the designated pee and poo area. Try this only after you are comfortable with using just one hand to maintain the slight steady tension on the leash.

4. Upon reaching the designated area, lose the pace, stop the chatter, slacken the leash, relax and enjoy the 'pee-poo dance'!

5. Once pee and/or poo has successfully made an appearance on the ground, praise and reward. Weather permitting, spend some time with Pup outside for play and fun (read why in paragraph 'Why play after each outdoor soiling session?'). Mission accomplished.

Please note that Pup may need some extra time to do his business outside, especially if he was abruptly interrupted indoors by your eager attempt to bring him out. Make apparent that there is no hurry to get back in—even if this is not completely true. If you are already late for work try taking a big breath to help you lose some of the stress and tension.

As tempting as it seems to just open the door to the garden to let Pup out to do his business alone while you wait for him indoors, this will not work.

4.7 The 'Exit Protocol'—Meet Molly

I was unlucky. My puppy, Molly, arrived in winter! December to be exact. Nothing will put into perspective the responsibilities of dog-ownership better than a winter housebreaking protocol! It is brutal; that I can assure you. There is nothing more inconvenient than having to rush out of bed, half asleep, into a frozen, rainy, snowy, windy night, and to have to wait there for as long as it takes for Pup to pee, only to have to do it all over again a couple of hours later, often without any result other than a nasty bout of the flu. But if I, a working mother of two (humans) with eight other animals to care for, can do it, so can anybody. As hard as it is, you mustn't focus on your discomfort but rather on the result: a fully house-trained Pup for the rest of your happy life together. The means most definitely justify the end, in our case.

Just like I did with Molly, it is very important that you also accompany your Pup. He needs the company and the guidance that only *you* can provide. You must keep going out with him into the cold, into the rain, and into feeling. You must also wait patiently and praise when pee or poo happens. As tempting as it seems to just open the door to the garden to let Pup out to do his business while you wait for him in the warmth and comfort of the indoors, *this will not work*. If you do not actually see him in the act of soiling, you run the risk of missing the most crucial moment in conveying the correct behaviour-altering message. It is the reward at the moment of release that signifies the correct place to soil: *outside*. Furthermore, if he is put outside in a rushed manner, i.e., a little bit more forcefully than normal, we risk giving Puppy the wrong impression: that he is being punished by being excluded from the rest of the family. This may lead Puppy to form a negative association related to the outdoors, and consequently, toilet confusion that may, possibly, in the long run, lead to incomplete housebreaking.

The answer to making so many unexpected outings as bearable as possible is to be prepared at all times (and for all weather conditions). We are, therefore, very excited to share with you our famous 'Exit Protocol':

The 'Exit Protocol' technique

Regardless of the weather conditions, we have to make sure that we are able to stay outside calmly for as long as it takes Pup to do his business, and ideally for a little longer - for a reinforcing short play session. Hurrying to get back inside will create tension at this sensitive time, allowing negative associations related to soiling to easily form. For swift, calm exits we will therefore need:

1. A coat (with house keys already in the pocket), shoes that you can slip on easily, a leash with poo bags already attached to it, and an umbrella (if winter). These should all be right by the door at all times, waiting for us to quickly grab on the way out. If you have multiple exits then these accessories should be available at each exit (!), or right by the bed, during the night.
2. If it is cold out, make sure that you are dressed warmly all day just in case you need to rush out unexpectedly into the freezing cold. A good idea is to keep shoes on all day. Puppy will not usually wait for you to find and put on your shoes!
3. If you are the absent-minded type, we recommend you wear your house key on a lanyard around your neck during the day. We have often found ourselves—together with Pup—locked out in the cold with no means to re-enter the house.

On the upside, the key lanyard also allows you to wear comfortable clothes without pockets, such as pyjamas and overalls.

4. If it is winter, consider having a hat, gloves and scarf always stuffed in a small rucksack next to your coat (or in the coat's pockets if they fit) as you never know how long you will need to be out until pooing or peeing is complete.

5. Keep treats handy in both your clothing pockets, your coat pockets and exit protocol rucksack.

6. Keep a towel by the door so that you can wipe muddy feet—yours and Puppy's!—on the way back in.

As hard as it is, you mustn't focus on your discomfort but rather on the result: a fully house-trained Pup for the rest of your happy life together.

4.8 Meet Campari, the worst case puppy pee-er!
By Klea Morianou

Campari arrived on the scene during the writing of this book. His timing was perfect because we had a live subject to play with. Little did I know how much of a challenge Campari would prove to be—my first acquaintance with a 30 TPD (times per day) Puppy pee-er!

If you have not met a constant pee-er, then consider yourselves extremely lucky.

The 30 TPD peeing puppy

If you have not met a constant pee-er, then consider yourselves extremely lucky! When Campari moved in with me—not so long ago—I was in for a big surprise: the two-month-old puppy was peeing 30 times per day (no exaggeration!). He proved to be one of the greatest peeing challenges I have ever had to deal with in all of my canine loving years. First of all, Campari had been trained to pee on pads which, for reasons already mentioned (see paragraph '4.3 Puppy training pads; A short term light relief'), made things more difficult. Every time he moved in the house, I knew in my gut that he was about to pee, but was never sure when.

Let's do some enlightening calculations. Campari slept 12-15 hours per day. To figure out his peeing frequency, divide the time he was awake by 30 (the number of times he peed during the day while awake) and you will find that Campari would pee three times per hour when he was awake. That means roughly every 20 minutes! As if this wasn't enough, he developed a preference for clean pads so he would not soil twice on the same one. As a result, pads kept getting thrown out after each use. This behaviour was getting very expensive!

I was fortunate to be able to take Campari to the office with me daily. Apart from the luxury of having his company all day, this meant I was able to constantly observe him, and gave me the opportunity to shape his peeing schedule. If you also have the opportunity to take your canine friend to work, I highly recommend that you do. It makes a world of difference.

At the office, I had made sure that there were training pads everywhere in the small space, that also happened to house another five not-so-amused, employees. Campari's constant peeing, each bout increasing exponentially in volume as he grew, was being reinforced by the training pads, and was generally becoming an inconvenience. So, the use of pads had to be terminated ASAP. The only alternative that entered my mind was to try a widely used technique (see paragraph the 'Umbilical Cord' technique) that I always use when an adult rescue-dog first enters my home. It required tethering Campari to my foot so as to restrict movement and, therefore, allow me to fully control him. Surprisingly, not only did it work, but within the space of only one week, he went from a 30 TPD pee-er to a 15 TPD pee-er. Peeing was reduced by 50% within a week, just by tethering Campari to my ankle. This was great.

You may ask, *"so why didn't I use a crate?"* since crates are recommended as such great tools for training puppies. The answer is *"I did!"*… and it didn't work. Not every technique is for every dog. Each dog is different.

You may ask, "so why didn't I use a crate?" The answer is "I did!"… and it didn't work. Not every technique is for every dog. Each dog is different.

Why crating does not work for 30 TPD pee-ers?

Crating helps a puppy learn to hold at first, and to improve holding capacity over time. The main problems I faced when trying to crate-train Campari were:

▶ The mere frequency of peeing bouts was so extreme that I was never quite sure whether he actually wanted to pee again, since he was just out and peeing (this is actually the definition of a double pee-er; and Campari was that too!), or was a ploy to get me to interact with him and open his crate. It was difficult, therefore to tell and to act. So what does one do? Stay indifferent to his barking and/or whining as one would have to do if it was an attention seeking ploy? Or take him out again, risking giving in to incessant whining that would aid in the formation of attention-seeking behaviours? A tough call to make. If you make the wrong call and *don't* open up the crate to let him out, Pup will end up eventually soiling his crate, something that will render the crate useless and his notification calls for help also useless. He will subsequently stop notifying and just soil in the crate *even* during the night.

▶ Excessive crating. Such a frequent pee-er means extended crating times which, as already mentioned, is a welfare issue (see paragraph '4.2 Crates, pens and spatial restriction'). He would be deprived of his freedom, his play time; he would miss out on familiarization with the home and office environment and most importantly, his interaction with me would be minimal at this very sensitive life stage—at least until he learned to hold his pee, that is.

What is a 'double pee-er'?

Scenario: Pup has successfully just peed outdoors. What an accomplishment! After celebrating, we bring him in and decide to safely lie back for half an hour while giving him the opportunity to explore the inside of the house—we've both earned it, after all. Oops... To our dismay, an extra pee occurs indoors only minutes after re-entering. How is this possible? What did we do wrong?

Some puppies or dogs do not fully relieve themselves in just one batch; they need an extra pee in order to fully empty their bladder. This is our definition of a double (or triple) pee-er. Knowing that your dog is a double pee-er can help prevent many soiling accidents—inside the house or crate—and avoid human confusion (and frustration).

Some extra time outdoors for play, after the initial pee, gives a double pee-er the opportunity to take his second indispensable pee in the right place. Good observation outdoors afterwards will help us detect this peculiarity.

4.9 Graduating to adult toilet savoir vivre

Common questions eagerly asked by guardians are: "How long will it take for Pup to go from the classic two-month-old puppy schedule of 12 outings a day to the normal adult schedule of two to three outings a day?" and "How is this achieved?".

Good questions. This is the tricky part. It takes time to establish a normal adult schedule and it occurs gradually while pup grows and gains increasingly more control over his sphincter muscles. As already mentioned, this sometimes long and arduous process requires spatial restriction, in combination with perfect cooperation between both parties—human and dog. It requires an open channel of communication and each party to be tuned in. Most responsibility, however, lies with the human, owing to maturity (in most cases) and the fact that he is asking something unnatural of the dog (see paragraph '1.2 Brave new world'). It is our responsibility to be constantly on the ball and able to feel: 1) when Pup really needs to go out, and 2) when Pup is able to go that one step further and hold on for a little longer. If you *do* feel that he is able to hold on a little longer, increase the time intervals between outings by half an hour every few days. Always, however, do so according to the messages you are getting from Pup. Pup's responsibility, in return, is to come up with a way to communicate to his human 'when he needs to go'.

This time is, in my opinion, the hardest one of all, and one when troubleshooting is likely to be required. How long will it take? Nobody knows. If the human is impeccable in his toilet-training abilities—which is rarely the case—then it is a matter of just waiting for Pup to mature and make that all important 'click' in his head. This 'click' happens at different times for each pup. You can almost feel it when it does. Pup suddenly comes to a realisation: *"Oh, so that is what I am supposed to do"*. It is quite exciting when it happens. Equally, the human must also come to a realisation of his own: recognising when Pup 'needs to go'. This happens when Pup figures out how to tell you that he wants to relieve himself by either whining or standing by the door or both. Yet, until synchronicity is reached, it *is* a bumpy ride. Accidents are likely to happen and it is important that when they do, you do not overreact and instead try to handle the situation appropriately so that attention seeking doesn't ensue (see paragraph '6.3 Attention seeking behaviour').

Finally, please note that as important as it is to make sure you are taking Pup out on time, it is equally important to not take him out too often—especially after the 'click' has occurred. Ideally, the frequency of outings has to be just at that point where Pup's physical ability to hold himself exactly equals the time that he has learned to hold himself. If you take him out too often, he will never experience the 'holding' part, and so will never train his sphincter muscles to hold; or he might have difficulty making the association in his head that *"When I need to go; I feel a physical need to go; I must go outside"*.

As important as it is to make sure you are taking him out on time, it is equally important to not take him out too often—especially after the 'click' has occurred.

CHAPTER 5

When does a natural puppy-hood trait become a proper problem behaviour?

So when does disorderly puppyhood soiling cease to be a natural developmental phase of growing dogs? When does soiling in the house actually become a behavioural problem? Unfortunately, more often than not; a lot sooner than when we actually recognise it.

5.1 Identifying the problem

First things first. Does your dog, or your client's dog, actually have a potty problem? According to the American Humane Society, generally speaking, a puppy can control their bladder one hour for every month of age. So if your puppy is two months old, he can hold it for about two hours. Taking this statement as fact, even though my experience tells me that this is rarely the case (two-month old puppies usually need to pee a lot more often than every two hours), let's make the relevant calculations. Assuming our day has 16 hours (starts at 7am and ends at 11pm) and we consider housebreaking to be achieved when Pup can hold himself long enough to be going out as frequently as an adult dog i.e., three times during that day, then 16 divided by three gives us 5.3 hours. If one hour is equivalent to one month of age, this means that puppy is considered housebroken at 5.3 months of age. This statement is, from my experience, generally true; after all, even Campari (see paragraph '4.8 Meet Campari, the worst case Puppy pee-er!') managed to make it. However, for some puppies, it is still definitely wishful thinking. The truth is that every puppy is different. There is breed and size to consider and then individuality on top of that. Smaller breeds mature faster than larger breeds and so should, in theory, be quicker and easier to train, but because they pee such tiny amounts, and a lot more often, it is much more challenging to housetrain a Yorkshire Terrier than a Labrador. In fact, we believe that many small breed culprits go unnoticed for years purely because the amount of pee they leave behind is so small.

There are a lot of factors to consider, but for the sake of facilitating things let's generalise and assume the above to be true. As a general rule, therefore, we can state that:

'A dog with a toileting behavioural problem is any dog that is over six months of age and not consistently using the outdoors as a toilet, opting, whether frequently or infrequently, to do his business indoors'.

If your dog, according to this definition, has a potty problem, then it is your duty as his human guardian to help eliminate it as soon as possible because the longer he continues to behave in this way, the less chances you have of eliminating the problem and the more of a welfare issue it will become. Chances are you are also dealing with anxiety, making things much harder. Plus, I'm sure that mopping up pee and poo, or having to wash beds and furniture for the next fifteen years of your shared life together, is not going to help your relationship. This is something that we really don't want to see happen.

How and why did your dog lose its way to the outdoors?

Solving any problem, including adolescent or adult dog toilet trouble, requires an understanding of:

1. The underlying cause
2. The mechanism driving the behaviour

An understanding of the underlying cause will give us an idea of *why* it started to begin with i.e., what was it, right at the start, that caused Dog to change his toileting ways? Finding the cause is just the tip of the iceberg though. More important is to understand the mechanism behind the behaviour in the now. In other words, what this new behaviour means for the dog and how he benefits from it today? How is it being reinforced? What is feeding the behaviour?

This will give us the *how* this behaviour has become a habit and continues to be used by the dog. Only by understanding the underlying cause and mechanism driving the behaviour will we gain insight on how to deal with it in order to extinguish it.

The truth is that every puppy is different. There is breed and size to consider and then individuality on top of that.

To complicate things further, each case of adult toilet trouble is usually a multi-dimensional problem with more than one cause and more than one benefit to the animal involved. The purpose of this book is not to categorise and then later outline all the possible causes and benefits. Each dog, and therefore each case, is entirely unique in its nature. This is an impossible and pointless task. What is important is for you to get an understanding of the general nature of these problems. This knowledge is enough (with some further investigation on your part into the intricacies of your dog's own unique take on things) to be able to help you understand and then later deal with his toileting issues. The following general causes (see 'Chapter 6: Causes of adult toilet trouble') can be mixed and matched in any number of combinations in order to give you the full behavioural 'diagnosis' of your own dog's problem. Please refer to our 'Self-diagnosis Flow Chart' in Appendix B for some visual guidance.

*To complicate things further,
each case of adult toilet trouble is
usually a multi-dimensional
problem with more than one
cause and more than one benefit
to the animal involved.*

It can be harder to re-train an adult than to start fresh with a puppy because the unwanted persistent behaviour must become unlearnt.

5.3 What's next?

So Dog, previously known in his immature state as Puppy, is now over six months of age, and has a toilet problem i.e., peeing or pooing in the house. First step, and the most crucial one at that, is a trip to the vet to rule out any underlying medical problem that may exist, especially if the problem started suddenly and seemingly without cause. If the cause isn't medical, then it is behavioural and most probably, in my experience, an incomplete housebreaking issue. As part of his rehabilitation, therefore, Dog will probably end up needing to undergo some sort of toilet housebreaking training again, much like Pup did, in order to correct the behaviour. In other words, he will need to be re-programmed by re-training.

This is especially true if Dog has been behaving like this for a long time and there is a large learnt component. The longer he behaves 'inappropriately', the larger the learnt component and the harder it is to correct. So, in some cases, it can be harder to re-train an adult than to start fresh with a puppy because the unwanted persistent behaviour must become unlearnt and the involved emotions addressed. Additionally, if it has also become a coping mechanism of some sort so that it, in some way, benefits the dog, and as a consequence is, very rewarding for him, then his perception of it must also be altered.

Peeing and pooing in the house feels good

It can be very rewarding for Dog if it:
1. Relieves stress
2. Attracts human attention
3. Serves to mark territory

CHAPTER 6

Causes of adult toilet trouble

Soiling problems are complex and have many causes. However, the major causes of inappropriate elimination are: incomplete housebreaking; urine marking; attention seeking; anxiety disorders such as separation anxiety; submissive urination; excitement or greeting urination; and inappropriate elimination because of underlying medical problems. Remember that before turning to a behavioural explanation, it is vital that all medical causes be ruled out, so it is advised that your first port of call be your vet. For the purposes of this book, we are going to concentrate solely on the behavioural causes and leave the medical ones in the hands of your very capable vet.

6.1 Revenge: A wrong cause

Before delving into the different behavioural causes of inappropriate elimination, it is important to understand how and why the most commonly believed cause, *revenge*, isn't actually a cause at all. We believe that revenge is simply something that dogs, due to their incredible nature, are incapable of attempting. They emphasise the moment, the here and now, and do not spend their time scheming behind our backs on how to get back at us, although they probably *should* in some cases! They are much more sophisticated than that. If they soil inside the house—either in your presence or when you are away—and even if they look 'guilty' upon your return, it is more likely an expression of an underlying emotion rather than payback. Revenge is something that simply doesn't exist in the dog world.

Remember that before turning to a behavioural explanation, it is vital that all medical causes be ruled out, so it is advised that your first port of call be your vet.

6.2 Incomplete housebreaking

Incomplete housebreaking is exactly what its name suggests: incomplete learning of how and when to soil properly and completely. It is, in my experience, the initial cause of most evolving toileting problems in adult dogs. In other words, most dogs displaying inappropriate soiling habits in adulthood have not, in puppyhood, learned fully and completely how and where to go to the toilet. Additionally, it is one of the trickiest causes to diagnose even though it is one of the most common of all the causes.

Why is it so hard to detect? For two reasons. Firstly, because it is difficult for the untrained guardian to perceive how an adult dog's soiling problem could actually stem from years ago when he was just a puppy. One focuses on what is triggering the problem now, and not what triggered it to begin with, in the past. Secondly, few people actually know the full proper housebreaking process and so knowledge that does not exist cannot be questioned.

Let's look at a common scenario:

A guardian puts down a training pad and, as I have often found, expects Puppy to know instinctively that he must go to the toilet on the training pad. It is as if Puppy was born with the knowledge *"we pee and poo **only** on the white square area within the two-legged animals' dens"*.

This assumption leads to the guardians' neglect in guiding their puppy properly. Instead of taking Puppy to the pad often during the day, and waiting with him quietly and patiently, then rewarding Puppy when he relieves himself, the human will take Puppy two-to-three times per day, or whenever he/she remembers, and, if Pup happens by chance to use the pad correctly, will give him a pat and a *"good boy"*.

Conversely, if he doesn't use it correctly and the human discovers the urine or faeces around the house—even a while after Puppy has actually done it—the guardian will make a point of making a much bigger fuss by scolding and punishing Puppy for doing such an unimaginable thing as soiling the house. This is a human approach to teaching and learning and is very far from anything a canine would understand. Not only do they not understand it, but it is counterproductive and will serve to initiate anxiety and further unwanted attention seeking behaviour (see paragraph '6.3 Attention seeking behaviour'), which will result in a nasty and confusing vicious cycle of persistent house soiling.

Conclusively—as a result of the guardian's lack of a) understanding of canine learning, b) housebreaking experience, and c) effort—Puppy, purely by chance, will only half-learn to use the training pads. He ends up soiling on them sometimes and at other times—either because he missed or because it was just convenient to soil elsewhere—intentionally and intermittently continues to soil the floor. The ultimate result is that soiling the floor never becomes forbidden in his little mind, and this perception, if not changed, will be carried on into adulthood. As the dog grows, the problem also grows and generalizes. He never learns completely to hold his bladder as he can freely pee wherever he gets the urge to.

Most dogs displaying inappropriate soiling habits in adulthood have not, in puppyhood, learned fully and completely how and where to go to the toilet.

Treating incomplete housebreaking

The most effective way to treat incomplete house-breaking is to prevent Dog from soiling in the house, while reprogramming him from scratch. If Dog is never given the opportunity to soil in the house, he will quickly learn to soil only outside, provided you simultaneously implement a successful training program much like the housebreaking protocol described in Chapter 4. Such protocols require Dog to be taken to an appropriate location for soiling on a regular schedule, while using positive reinforcement (a reward) to mark the required behaviour (the moment he eliminates in the desired location). It is vital to provide constant supervision when Dog is loose in order to prevent house soiling, either by vigilant observation or by attaching Dog to us with a lead, a technique otherwise referred to as the 'Umbilical Cord' technique. If, at any point, we are not able to provide supervision and he is untethered, Dog must be restricted to his own space, i.e., crate or room or somewhere where soiling is allowed, for example his own outdoor run.

The most effective way to treat incomplete housebreaking is to reprogramme Dog from scratch all the while preventing him from soiling in the house.

The 'Umbilical Cord' technique

This technique requires a 1.5 to 2-meter lead connecting Dog to our ankle when we are in a seated or lying position (computer work, studying, reading etc.). A somewhat longer 2 to 2.5-meter lead connecting Dog to our waist or belt is needed when standing up (e.g., when cooking or ironing). Dog needs to be able to move freely and get into a comfortable sleeping position at all times. He needs to be able to change sides, sit or stand at will.

This method replaces vigilant observation, allowing us to go ahead with our daily tasks without depriving Dog and ourselves of each other's presence. Furthermore, Dog is already wearing his lead, which is extremely handy and much faster, guaranteeing a speedy exit when the need arises.

Each small shake or tug of the lead initiated by Dog while getting up is a possible alarm that may signal a need to soil. In this case, we take Dog to an appropriate location for soiling, observe his behaviour—looking specifically for the pee-poo dance: sniffing the ground, circling around himself, lowering the back end of his body etc. We wait patiently. Once he pees or poos—if he does—we reward.

It is important to note here that tethering may increase the risk of separation anxiety if a) Dog is tethered to you all day long and b) while Dog is tethered to you, you take this opportunity to constantly turn your attention towards him and make him the center of your world. Make sure that even though he is so close to you during these times, you are aloof and preoccupied with other things. The tethering is used merely to prevent him from wandering away to pee; not for your constant attention.

Attention-seeking behaviour patterns include any behaviour that the dog finds rewarding and that attracts positive, or even negative, attention from its guardians.

6.3 Attention-seeking behaviour

Attention-seeking behaviour is one of the most common canine behavioural problems today and by far the biggest category of dog behaviour problems. Why category? Because attention-seeking behaviours are many and are very varied.

Dogs, as a result of domestication, have become more and more anthropocentric, so their desire for attention has greatly increased. This is especially true of purebred dogs. Consequently—and in conjunction with our increasingly busy lifestyles, which serve to take us away from our dogs for increasingly longer periods of time every day—a wide variety of attention-seeking behaviour patterns can form and it is very difficult to name them all. These patterns include *any* behaviour that the dog finds rewarding and that attracts positive, or even negative, attention from its guardians.

Additionally, they can be very tricky to 'diagnose' as their conspicuousness varies in each circumstance.

They can be blatantly obvious, like persistent jumping and barking in your face, and yet extremely ambiguous, like secretly soiling inappropriately while the human is away in order to attract his attention upon his return home. I also find that any attention-seeking behaviour can surface either as a primary behavioural problem or as a secondary one, whereby it enhances and drives the primary one. Although attention-seeking behaviour can be very problematic, it is also important to keep in mind that both we and our dogs engage in a little harmless attention-getting behaviour from time to time, and there's nothing particularly wrong with that—as long as the behaviour stays within reasonable limits. We want our dogs to be able to say *"Hey, come here I want to show you something"* by giving us a bark that we respond to. This is within the context of healthy communication.

Attention-seeking behaviour is a huge topic for discussion but, for the purpose of this book, it is important to concentrate on problem attention-seeking behaviour related to peeing and pooing. More specifically, we want to know how inappropriate elimination becomes attention-seeking and how to deal with it, should it arise.

Since time has elapsed from the moment your dog soiled, the chance to correct the behaviour has passed. Your best bet is, therefore, to just let it pass without adding misplaced emphasis.

Who is to blame?

It all starts when we humans begin to scold and punish our dogs at the wrong time and in the wrong way, much like we unfortunately often do our own children. This approach during the puppy-stage—the most mischievous and exuberant of all life stages—would mean *non-stop scolding*. At this stage, Puppy is grabbing and chewing on everything and still also soiling uncontrollably. Taking on a corrective approach would therefore merely result in too much attention on Pup while he is engaged in inappropriate and unwanted behaviours.

Conversely, as is usually the case, when he is calm and quietly sleeping in his bed, he is ignored in an attempt to avoid more energetic and destructive outbursts. This leads the dog to, quite rightly, associate our attention with unwanted behaviours and so continues to do them so that we will interact with him. Dogs learn by forming associations in their heads and so this example can apply to any behaviour that attracts too much attention at the wrong time, including soiling behaviour. One such association, commonly formed, if one scolds upon finding a mess hours later, could be:

"The presence of pee or poo on my human's carpet, when he returns home, turns his attention to me".

Notice that, by scolding upon our return, it is the *presence* of the poo or pee that is associated with your *negative attention*, and not the act of soiling that occurred hours before. Timing here is the important factor. Since time has elapsed from the moment your dog deposited its offering, *the chance to correct the behaviour has passed*. Your best bet is, therefore, to just let it pass without adding misplaced emphasis.

I very often hear from my clients, in an attempt to dispute this when I am explaining it to them, something like this: *"But he knows he has done something wrong. The minute I walk in he cowers and runs to hide"*. If you are seeing this in your dog, it is because he is picking up on your anxious anticipation of discovering the mess and reading your aggressive facial expression and body language as you are scanning the house to find the mess. He is not being *"guilty"* or *"sorry"* about something that he did hours ago. He is reacting to you now. A very attention-hungry dog, that is also generally under-stimulated, will see this whole 'poo and pee discovery ritual' as a game, and you will often see the dog actively following and observing their guardian while he/she anxiously scans the house for pee or poo and this game in itself is what feeds the behaviour. It provides them with stimulation and something to anticipate in their boring day.

How does inappropriate soiling escalate into attention-seeking soiling?

There are so many different scenarios that can take place, but for the sake of simplicity let's take one of many, the most common, as an example. Dog is peeing and pooing intermittently outside or on the training pad indoors, as a result of incomplete housebreaking (see paragraph '6.2 Incomplete housebreaking'). We are either working long hours or are not vigilant enough within the home, so we do not catch him in the act. Every time we discover the mess—either upon returning home or merely by moving between rooms in the house—our blood begins to boil and we make noises of frustration. We then seek out the culprit and angrily bring him back to the scene, all the while making a big fuss and muttering to ourselves, *"What have you done here again? How many times have I told you not to do*

this? I'm fed up with this day in and day out! Bad dog, bad dog". To make matters worse we simultaneously actively point to the pee or poo, or, as is shamefully done in some cases, even rub the animal's nose in it.

This attempt at discipline, even though obviously unsuccessful, continues long term into adolescence and then, in some cases adulthood. The result? A very confused, anxious and stressed animal that still has no idea that what he is doing is wrong. The only thing that Dog has learnt by association is that *we pay attention to him mostly with the presence of urine or faeces on the floor,* and so he makes it his mission to continue to please himself in this way.

The lack of daily mental and physical stimulation that Dog is likely subjected to—due to our long hours at work or our busy daily lifestyle—doesn't help. An under-stimulated and bored dog will spend his energy in mischievous ways that, although are satisfying to him, are usually unwanted by us. In other words, a dog learns that this ritual, in the long run, provides him with the much needed attention and stimulation that he craves; and so he continues to replicate it.

If Dog soils in the house and you don't catch him in the act, the most productive thing to do is to clean it up without, however, an eager spectator.

Treating attention-seeking elimination

The only way to eliminate any kind of attention-seeking behaviour is to *remove all attention and emphasis* from either the act itself, or the results of the act, i.e., the pee or poo deposits. If Dog finds it 'amusing' to soil in front of you, in anticipation of a chase, then simply do not indulge in a chase! In fact, you must completely ignore it. This means *no eye or verbal contact at that moment when it is most wanted*.

If Dog soils in the house and you don't *catch him in the act*, then there is really nothing that you can do at that time. The most productive thing to do is to clean it up *without*, however, *an eager spectator*. Wait until Dog is otherwise occupied and clean up without him noticing you. Additionally, all search rituals must cease. It is important for you to relax regarding Dog's soiling problem and to *stop* intentionally, anxiously and tensely scanning the house for deposits. If you happen to come across a little 'treasure', just ignore it and wait for the correct moment, i.e., when your dog isn't watching, to clean it up.

If Dog finds it 'amusing' to soil in front of you, in anticipation of a chase, then simply do not indulge in a chase! In fact, you must completely ignore it.

The 'Fleece Technique': Keeping cool when shit happens

You are in the process of fixing Dog's pee habits and you will manage, eventually, to do so. Meanwhile, you really need to try and stay calm every time you discover a puddle of pee, even if it is in the most unsuitable place and even if it happened at the most inappropriate moment in time—usually when you are in a rush or you are ready to call it a night.

You must know by now that the most absorbent furnitures are usually popular targets and the hardest to handle: beds, carpets and upholstery. The 'Fleece Technique' is not suited for carpets but can help protect his bed, your mattress, couch or favorite armchair. All you will need are training pads and fleece blankets (the thicker the better). Place the training pads first on the surface you wish to protect and then at least two fleece blankets (folded twice) on top of the training pads.

Try to use them to cover all the places Dog has wet in the past, or the ones you suspect that he intends to, in the future. We know that many of you avoid fleece products as they tend to attract and trap hair, but there are some advantages. They are extremely absorbent, easy to wash and, strangely, they dry in an instant, which make them easy to clean and reuse after each soiling accident. But what should interest you most is that they tend to trap water. Their amazing hydrophilic property rarely allows for pee to leak through to the training pads beneath. Your furniture is, therefore, now safe.The earlier you discover the spill, however, the better. As soon as you discover the accident, remove the fleece cover, wash it (not forgetting to also use enzymatic cleaner) and replace it with a clean, dry one.

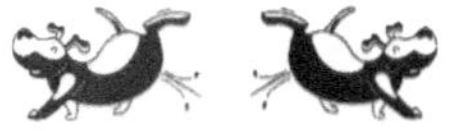

Why are purebreds usually more attention seeking?

1. They have been selectively bred to be more anthropocentric, i.e., dogs that were closest to humans were—and are—the ones chosen to breed, creating an escalation of this trait with the passage of years.
2. They are always born into human hands. One of the first things that they encounter is human energy so they are immediately imprinted onto humans.

Marking is a dog's way of communicating with the world around him and claiming territory. It is only in the human world— and mainly when expressed within the home—that this behaviour is considered disgusting and unacceptable.

6.4 "I mark, therefore I am"

Inappropriate urination can start suddenly upon reaching sexual maturity by both males and females. It is, therefore, a result of hormonal changes in their body. This can happen anywhere between six months to one year of age. It is, however, usually the unneutered males that will mark most prominently due to the increased levels of testosterone that serve to trigger the need to claim territory and to signal sexual availability to the females.

Marking behaviour is, therefore, a dog's way of communicating with the world around him and claiming territory. It is a normal instinctive behaviour in the dog world and has a distinct function, making it very difficult to treat. It is only in the human world—and mainly when expressed within the home—that this behaviour is considered disgusting and unacceptable.

When marking, a dog will usually deposit smaller amounts of pee or poo on anything that he wants to claim. On the walk you will notice that your dog will likely seek out and urinate over other dogs' urine, and the males will make it a point to lift their legs as high as possible, sometimes even standing on their two front legs, in an attempt to deposit their urine above all other deposits. What they are trying to say is: *"This tree is mine"* or *"I have been here and I am bigger than you"*. Conversely, if Dog is not peeing outside normally and prefers the indoors to the outdoors, i.e., is peeing upon returning home, then he is likely—if not displaying a substrate preference—to be insecure about leaving his scent outside and exposing himself to the other animals in the neighbourhood. *He is actually hiding.*

Inside the house, dogs with a marking problem may put their stamp on anything that is important to them, such as toys, food and water bowls, chews and beds. Additionally, they will show special preference to whatever is carrying novel scents, i.e., novel objects that enter the house, shopping bags, shoes, guests and even their own guardians. However, it is important to note that dogs who start marking within their home environment are frequently responding to stress or anxiety that has been triggered by some sort of previous stressor. It is *not* done out of anger, jealousy, spite and so forth, as many wrongly believe. Some stressors that may trigger persistent and frequent marking may be: new additions to the family (either four-legged or two-legged), a change of house, new animals in the neighbourhood, a change in the humans' routine, a death in the family etc. Essentially, marking can be triggered by anything that makes the dog feel insecure and anxious.

Dogs who start marking within their home environment are frequently responding to stress or anxiety that has been triggered by some sort of previous stressor.

Treating marking behaviour

The ease with which you will be able to treat your dog's marking behaviour within the home is mostly reliant on how long he has been marking. The sooner you deal with it, the easier it will be to reverse this annoying habit. If your dog is over a year old, the first thing to consider is spaying or neutering. The quicker this is done, the better. Reducing the hormones that trigger marking will remove a major cause of this behaviour and in some cases, if done at the right time i.e., early on, it may be all you need to reverse the behaviour. However, if your dog has been marking for a while then there will also be a learnt component that will need to be dealt with.

The learnt component can be tricky and requires, first of all, a reprogramming of your dog's brain in order to unlearn the bad behaviour and replace it with a more acceptable one. This is done by carrying out much the same housebreaking routine that one would use to train a puppy (see 'Chapter 4: Complete housebreaking for puppies and adult dogs'). Back to the basics we go, therefore.

Additionally, it is important to clean soiled areas properly and to change the dog's concept of all the areas he was soiling before by either making them unattractive (covering them with tin foil or plastic sheets), inaccessible (placing large objects there), or changing them completely, e.g., if your dog was peeing in a certain corner then place his food or water bowl there to change that area to one of eating and drinking as opposed to one of soiling.

However, as with any problem behaviour, best results will be achieved if the root cause of the problem, *and not merely the symptom,* is addressed. Good observation is required to understand *why* your dog is being led to mark in the first place.

It is my experience, however, that anxiety is the root cause of 90% of all behaviour problems and so it is this nasty emotional state, and whatever is causing it—whether it be conflicts between animals or conflicts with humans, or any other change or trigger that the animal has been exposed to and which it perceives as a stressor—that must be dealt with first.

One of these triggers could be the moment that you exit the front door to leave and go to work, which brings us to our next cause, which is unfortunately a very common and difficult problem: separation anxiety.

Good observation is required to understand why your dog is being led to mark in the first place.

6.5 Separation anxiety

Dogs are social animals. They live in small family groups and their survival, especially when young, depends on the presence of other members of their group. Being alone in nature makes them vulnerable to predators and greatly reduces their chances of finding food. So being left alone in the house—usually for long hours every day while we work—is again another strange expectation of the human world and is something that a dog needs to be taught at a young age. If a dog misses this lesson, or for some reason—as is often the case with rescue animals—he experiences insecurity in the form of changes in family structure or multiple house moves, then this insecurity may manifest itself as a problem called 'separation anxiety'.

Being left alone in the house for long hours is again another strange expectation of the human world and is something that a dog needs to be taught at a young age.

So, what is it?

A dog exhibiting separation anxiety will not sit at home calmly in the absence of his guardian; instead he finds and does other, often humanly unacceptable things, to relieve the stress caused by his absence. One of the many symptoms, and the most common, is uncontrolled urination and defecation in the house—but only while the human is away or out of sight or reach. Other symptoms include destruction of objects or furniture within the house, destruction of parts of the house (windows and door frames), and increased vocalisation—whining or barking constantly or intermittently—throughout the duration of the humans' absence. An additional feature of these dogs and a result of their insecurity is their tendency to attach themselves intensely to their humans. Their obsession with their human is so intense that they are commonly referred to as 'velcro dogs'. They are usually difficult to avoid, following and watching your every move within the house.

It is very important to understand the underlying emotion of a dog that exhibits separation anxiety as one of absolute anxiety and confusion. Most people wrongly believe that the dog is being vindictive and 'getting back' at them for leaving them alone. This is absolutely not the case. If you believe this, then it is natural that you will return home and become angry at the discovery of the mess, and your reaction will be one of harsh punishment as a means of correcting the problem. This way of dealing with the problem will only lead to more anxiety and the dog will become fearful of you, ultimately leading to a rupture in your bond with him. When Dog is acting like this, he is not feeling very well. He is disoriented and, as already mentioned, in a state of anxiety and stress. Consequently, he does not have complete control of his behaviour and in severe cases may lose all control.

Separation anxiety can become a serious clinical behaviour problem; 20-40% percent of dogs presented to veterinary behavioural specialists suffer from this disorder (College of Veterinary Medicine Illinois University, 2019). That is almost half the dogs that vets see. It is, in my opinion, not only one of the most common behaviour problems, but also the one that causes the greatest emotional discomfort to both the dog and his human. It can appear in dogs of any age or breed, and is one of the most common reasons for euthanasia or abandonment. It can reach extreme levels, resulting in serious household destruction or even self-injury to the teeth, the gums, the surrounding areas of the mouth, and the paws in a desperate attempt to escape the house to find their human.

Most people wrongly believe that the dog is being vindictive and 'getting back' at them for leaving them alone. This is absolutely not the case.

What made my dog start behaving this way?

It is still unclear why some dogs succumb to separation anxiety and others don't—even when they live under the same conditions. Research suggests that this problem has a genetic component since dogs with the problem usually have other neurological issues as well—such as extensive fears and phobias.

It has been generally observed that the nature of the relationship between most dogs with separation anxiety and their guardians is quite specific and worth noting. It seems that, in these cases, the guardian has, due to emotional deficit, replaced a human family member with their dog. As a consequence, these dogs are excessively cared for and this constant attention, in combination with the high emotional load that they endure, leads to over-dependence on the dogs' part. This dependence, as is to be expected, makes dealing with the guardian's absence much harder for the dog. The antithesis between being with his guardian and being alone becomes too big to bear as the house— an otherwise over-stimulating environment—suddenly becomes totally void of any kind of stimulation. Even in more balanced relationships, excessive care and attention can have a similar effect. Therefore, it is very important to be aware of our own personal needs that are being projected onto our animals so as not to become an emotional burden for them.

Some other triggers seem to be:

- A change of environment where the new living conditions are very different from the old ones.
- Early or late weaning i.e., before eight weeks and after three and a half months of age.
- Immediately after a period of spending more than the usual time together, e.g., a holiday.
- After a traumatic period away from home e.g., after staying in an animal hotel, shelter or at the vet.
- After a traumatic experience that caused the dog a lot of fear.
- A change in the guardian's working routine, e.g., returning or leaving at different hours than usual.
- Old age.
- Abandonment during critical developmental phases.
- A house move.
- A change in family structure, such as when a new animal or person enters the family, when a child leaves home to study or when there has been a death in the family.

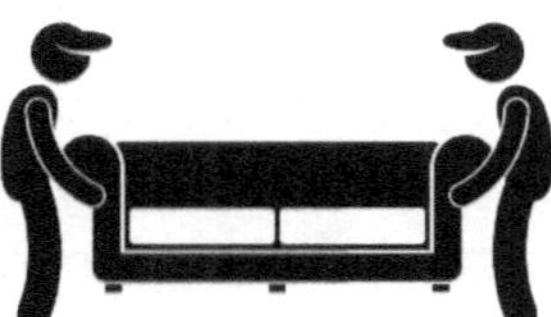

It is very important to be aware of our own personal needs that are being projected onto our animals so as not to become an emotional burden for them.

Any punishment at the time that Dog's mess (urine or faeces) is discovered will only lead to further confusion, more stress and consequently, to an escalation of the problem.

6.6 Treating separation anxiety related soiling

Any punishment at the time that Dog's mess (urine or faeces) is discovered will only lead to further confusion, more stress and consequently, to an escalation of the problem—since he will not make the association *"I am being scolded for what I did hours ago"* (see paragraph 'Who is to blame?' in '6.3 Attention seeking behaviour'). Correction can only be used on the spot and when Dog is caught in the act (see '2.2 How to act when dog is caught in the act') in order to avoid stress and to prevent the behaviour from becoming an attention-seeking tool. However, since Dog relieves himself in our absence, it is unlikely that we will catch him in the act. So what do we do?

Firstly, since separation anxiety is related to high levels of stress and anxiety, our main goal should be to reduce these negative states of being. It is only possible to reach the mind of an animal and teach it new things if the nervous system is relaxed and open to communication. I achieve this with the help of natural alternative healing modalities such as Bach flower remedies, essential oils, and herbal tinctures. One such remedy, with a large spectrum of healing abilities, is Rescue Remedy. Once the physical aspect has been addressed and the animal is in the process of becoming calmer and more receptive, I then move on to behavioural techniques.

It is only possible to reach the mind of an animal and teach it new things if the nervous system is relaxed and open to communication.

The human factor

The hardest part, yet the most important in dealing with this problem, is to remain calm and to erase any feelings of guilt that you have about leaving him alone. Your anxiety and guilt can very easily affect your dog by way of empathy and can serve to fuel the whole situation. So firstly, take a deep breath and dissociate yourself from the problem. The calmer you are, the calmer he will become. Secondly, although very hard to do—but extremely vital—ignore anything that you discover upon returning home. Clean up the mess using an enzymatic cleaner to reduce all odours, and do this in the absence of your dog (see 'The Correct Cleaning Protocol' in '2.3 Proper cleaning of puddles and piles!'). Now you can move on to behavioural work.

Behaviour modification techniques

Behaviourally, you must reduce the emphasis that exists regarding your absence so as to pass the message *"I come and go and it is of no special importance or significance to you—just a normal occurrence"*. This is done by reducing the attention you give your dog immediately prior to and after your absence. So for 10-15 minutes before leaving and upon returning, do not acknowledge the presence of Dog i.e., pretend he is invisible. Remain calm and go about your business, either preparing to leave or settling in upon arrival, despite the fuss that he might be making. This is especially difficult in the beginning, when returning home. In an attempt to greet you, and due to Dog's nervous state, he will be jumping up and down uncontrollably. No matter the fuss, remain calm until he has settled. Once settled, you can call him to you, ask for a 'sit' and then give Dog as much attention as you like.

Additionally, it is important to recognise and make a list of the different triggers that may be initiating his anxiety.

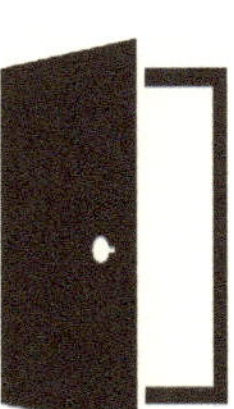

"I come and go and it is of no special importance or significance to you—just a normal occurrence."

Anxiety triggers

Any or all behaviours that *you* engage in before leaving the house could help initiate Dog's separation anxiety. Some common triggers are:

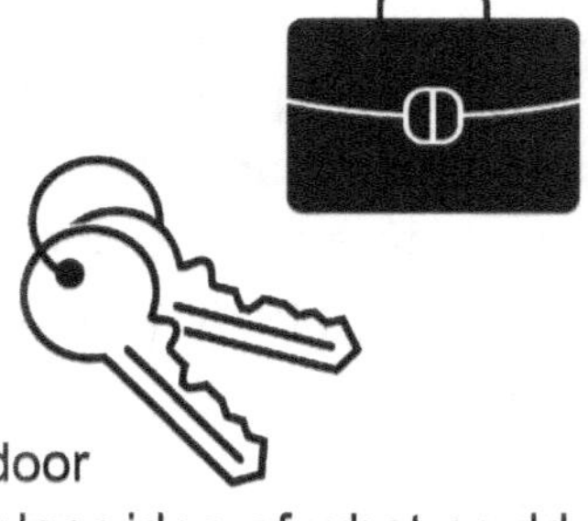

- Getting dressed
- Putting shoes on
- Taking keys
- Preparing bag
- Putting on coat
- Putting on hat
- Opening the front door

Once you have a clear idea of what could be triggering his anxiety, it is important to desensitize him to these triggers. This is done by repeating them many times during the day without them having the same outcome that they would usually have, i.e., you leaving. An example would be jiggling your keys many times during the day at random times so that he can hear the sound, but then put them in your pocket while continuing to do the laundry.

Mock leaving trials can be carried out many times daily. Get yourself ready to leave the house. Do all the behaviours that you would usually do before your exit, right up to opening the front door. Open the door then close it again and then go about your usual business within the house but still fully dressed to leave. You could sit on the sofa and watch TV in full outdoor dress—coat and hat on with bag in hand. He will look at you as if you are mad to begin with, but soon one would expect to see him react less and less until he is not bothered at all by your strange ritual.

Departure cues

Cues that mark your departure are important for dogs with anxiety. It helps them understand and prepare for what is about to happen, i.e., your leaving. I like to use a positive verbal cue myself. I say, *"Wait here and I'll be right back"*. I say this consistently for very small outings that don't bother the dog, to begin with, so that he can associate it with a calm state of mind. Examples of such outings could be when I go out onto the balcony, change rooms, take out the rubbish, or when I leave him in the car to quickly pop out to buy something.

Another example of a cue is a toy or chew stuffed with something yummy that will keep him busy for at least 15–20 minutes after you leave. A Kong is a great example of one such toy, and there are many great ideas on how to fill a Kong for this purpose on the internet. For the first two to three interactions with his Kong it is important that he gets it while in your presence so he is given the opportunity to get to know and love it carefree, before being left alone with it. This will empower the toy to keep Dog's attention later on when faced with the anxiety triggered by your absence. Once he has become familiar with his Kong, he gets it only while he is alone. It must be given to him immediately prior to you leaving the house and must be picked up immediately upon your arrival. With a toy such as this we are associating our departure with something very positive for him, thereby changing his perception and consequently his emotions related to being alone.

"Wait here and I'll be right back". I say this consistently for very small outings that don't bother the dog, to begin with, so that he can associate it with a calm state of mind.

Desensitisation techniques

The next and final step is desensitisation to your departure, and for this it is best that you seek professional guidance as it can be tricky, requiring *precision* in administering rewards so as not to create further anxiety. This is especially true if your dog is displaying advanced separation anxiety. However, a rough guideline, mainly for use with mild cases, would look something like this:

1. Have him *"sit"* and *"stay"* for short periods while you change rooms in the house. He should remain calmly seated when you are out of sight for those few minutes. You will need to build up the time gradually.

2. Have him *"sit"* and *"stay"* calmly while you approach the front door and grab the handle.

3. Have him *"sit"* and *"stay"* calmly while you open the front door and close it again.

4. Have him *"sit"* and *"stay"* calmly while you open the front door, take one step out (without closing the door) and then come back in

5. Have him *"sit"* and *"stay"* calmly while you open the door, take a step out, wait a few seconds (without closing the door) and then come back in.
6. Have him *"sit"* and *"stay"* calmly while you open the door, take a step out, close the door and immediately open it again.
7. Have him *"sit"* and *"stay"* calmly while you open the door, take a step out, close the door, wait five seconds and then open it and re-enter.

This final step should be repeated increasing the increments of time by five seconds, to begin with, gradually and as long as Dog is comfortable and calm. Once he can stay calmly for one minute, practice as many absences as possible, that last less than ten minutes.

Desensitisation to your departure can be tricky, requiring precision in administering rewards so as not to create further anxiety.

You can do many departures within one session if your dog remains calm between departures. Use his behaviour as a guide as to how fast or slow to proceed. If you see him get upset, then go back to the time interval that he was last happy with, remain there for a while and then proceed again to increasing it. Remember to keep your departures and entrances as neutral and calm as possible. You should do random practice departures and short-duration absences as much as possible throughout the day. Once Dog can handle short absences (30 to 90 minutes), he'll usually be able to handle longer intervals alone—without you having to increase the time gradually until he can be alone for many hours. The hard part is at the beginning. Nevertheless, you must go slowly at first. It gets easier as you go along. Remember, how long it takes to condition your dog to being alone depends on the severity of his problem. If you are struggling with this, please consult a professional.

What won't help

Spatial restriction—e.g., crates or safe rooms—is often used to deal with symptoms, i.e., physically preventing the dog from soiling or destroying the house. If used with this intention it will not work and his welfare will be compromised. Crates must not be used as a way to eliminate symptoms, but more as a training tool and with the intention to create a safe haven for the anxious animal. Anxious animals often take well to crates provided they are desensitised to them first, because they mimic the den for them. Neglecting to desensitise, however, will result in a worse panic-stricken reaction from Dog, causing many more problems.

Another misconception is that a dog that has separation anxiety needs the company of another dog. Please note that getting another animal as a companion for your dog will, in most cases, not solve or even improve the problem, as many people wrongly assume. Your dog is fixated on you; this problem revolves around *your* relationship with your dog. Another being will not change this. It may even aggravate the problem as Dog attempts to cope with the new addition to the family.

If upon implementation of all the above the problem persists, then it is important to involve a professional animal behaviourist to help you with further behavioural techniques.

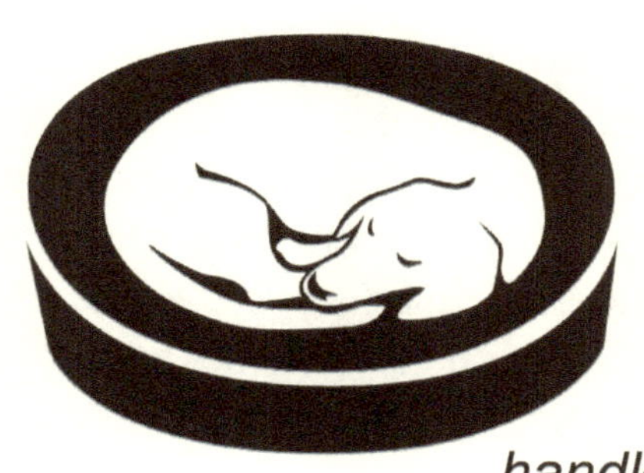

Once the dog can handle absences of 30 to 90 minutes, he'll usually be able to handle longer intervals alone.

6.7 Submissive urination

Does your dog leave unexpected little wet puddles all over the floor upon greeting you, meeting a stranger or approaching another dog? Is just a simple look from you, or anybody else, enough to create that little puddle? If so, it is very likely that you are witnessing either what is commonly termed as 'submissive urination', or a similar condition, 'excitement urination' (please also refer to next paragraph as the symptoms are very similar).

Submissive urination is a behaviour whereby a dog will deposit smaller than usual amounts of urine upon meeting his own human, a stranger, house guests, or another animal. It is a behaviour that is aimed at the appeasement of the upcoming person or animal and is expressed as a result of fear or stress related with the encounter. The dog is trying to communicate that he is not a threat; his aim is to increase the distance between himself and the approaching human or animal because he is *uncomfortable and afraid*. Urination will often be accompanied by other submissive or appeasing behaviours such as lowering of the body and head, lowering of the tail, and/or a submissive grin and lip licking.

A commonly misinterpreted behavioural problem

Contrary to common belief, submissive urination is a normal and useful behaviour in puppies as they learn to interact socially with their peers and the world around them. It should not, therefore, be a cause for any concern, as long as the behaviour fades away as the puppy grows and gains confidence and social aptness. Upon reaching adulthood there should be no traces left. If it doesn't subside, then it is important that steps be taken to help your dog gain more confidence around people before any learnt behaviour becomes a serious component of the equation.

Tips for dealing with submissive urination

1. Upon returning home, refrain from talking or greeting your dog until he is calm.
2. Ask any guests to also not greet your dog until he is calm.
3. Do not scold any form of submissive urination; this will only serve to increase fear and stress.
4. Do not reinforce any kind of excitable behaviour as excitement is also often associated with urination. Always pet and express love towards a calm dog.
5. Give your dog the choice to socially interact when he feels comfortable, by allowing him to approach when he feels confident to do so.
6. Any greetings should be made at the dog's own level to minimize the threat caused by towering over him. Lower your body when interacting and avoid eye contact.
7. Praise only confident behaviour.

6.8 Excitement urination

Excitement urination is exactly what the name suggests: urination triggered by a state of over-excitement. These times of over-excitement are usually also greeting moments with either humans or animals, so submissive and excitement urination are sometimes confused. The difference being that, during excitement, Pup's body language will be rather more upright with extreme tail wagging and more forward movement toward the upcoming human or animal than the more apprehensive submissive puppy would display. As puppies, they are usually both excited and submissive together, so some confusion is to be expected. But, as Pup grows, these behaviours should both fade away. If they don't, it then becomes more obvious which the underlying emotion actually is—submission or excitement. Either way, excitement behaviour is dealt with in much the same way as submissive urination; the dog is kept calm during greeting moments without excess energy and attention given to the dog. In fact, we do not give him any attention until he has completely calmed down.

CHAPTER 7
Soiling trouble in multi-pet homes

Multi-pet homes are different and special. I know this for a fact, after living in one for as long as I can remember. However, as amazing as they are, they are also deeply challenging, especially with regard to soiling, and so deserve a special mention in this book.

7.1 The multi-pet dynamic

In addition to all the humans of the family, within a multi-pet home one might find one or more dogs as well as other individuals of different species such as cats, rabbits, other rodents, and birds. Each individual carries its own species-specific blueprint of behaviours and characteristics, but also traits related to its own individual temperament, character and experiences. The accumulation of all these individuals creates a large fluctuating and interchangeable dynamic within the home, much like a vortex. I view this type of family as a living, breathing organism of its own, which can be affected in different ways depending on the balance and strength of the overall dynamic. Even minor events of everyday life—such as the return of a stressed human—can affect this dynamic.

The degree to which the dynamic will be affected is dependent on the balance within the dynamic. If the family is, in general, balanced, then each individual's reaction to stress and change, no matter the intensity, will be compensated for by the whole dynamic of the family and balance will be retained. If, however, the family is not in balance, then the dynamic will not be able to buffer out any tension and it will surface somewhere.

7.2 Insecurity within the dynamic

Tension and conflict will initially show their face within the relationships of the animals in the family and in varying degrees. One of the first signs with regards to dogs is sudden soiling of the house. The underlying emotion related to this sudden onset is *insecurity*. A dog's family is of paramount importance. In the wild, he would not be able to survive without it and so any threat would result first in an attempt to strengthen his tie to it. The individual dog feeling threatened will, therefore, initially proceed with marking his territory in order to strengthen his scent within it and consequently, his place within the family. He will most likely choose areas of high importance (such as beds, sofas) or belongings of his beloved humans (such as clothing) in an attempt to get closer to them. Also, any object entering the house is most likely to become a soiling target in an attempt to claim and mark it.

To conclude, if your dog's soiling problem started suddenly and you have a multi-pet household, it is a good idea, once a clean bill of health has been attained by a vet, to assume one of two possibilities:

1. Something generic has happened to create tension within the dynamic that is showing up as toilet trouble in the behaviour of *at least one* of the animals. You need to investigate what this might be.

2. Somehow the culprit is feeling insecure with regards to his place in the family. In this case, you need to investigate relationships.

In an attempt to solve the problem, we would first investigate the family as a whole and eliminate any perceived or actual threats, and then deal with making him feel secure again within it.

If the family is not in balance,
then the dynamic will not be able
to buffer out any tension and it
will surface somewhere.

7.3 Creating balance

The important aforementioned balance is created mainly by the humans of the family. To some it comes easier than others. Generally speaking, it is not a ride in the park and requires vigilance, increased awareness and empathy on behalf of the humans. We must be able to monitor the dynamic at all times and feel and know immediately when something is out of place. Quick steps must then be taken to bring about balance again.

Some general guidelines that can be followed by the humans in order to increase the chances of creating a balanced dynamic are:

- ▶ Creating calm within themselves.
- ▶ Creating calm within the house.
- ▶ Increasing empathy and intuition through meditation and other energy work.
- ▶ Keeping a positive outlook on life.
- ▶ Being a good and respected leader.
- ▶ Taking the time and energy to know each individual animal very well.
- ▶ Creating a 'home' whereby each individual's species-specific biological needs regarding space, exercise, stimulation, training, nutrition etc. are met.
- ▶ Providing enough space, time and energy for all.

The balance is created mainly by the humans of the family. To some it comes easier than others. Generally speaking, it is not a ride in the park and requires vigilance, increased awareness and empathy on behalf of the humans.

130

CHAPTER 8
Coprophagia: a disgusting habit for some

Coprophagia is the ingestion of one's own or another's excrement. Disgusting right? However, as disgusting as it may seem to us humans, the eating of faeces is widespread in the animal world. Among mammals it is commonly found in rodents, rabbits, beavers, elephants and non-human primates (Coren, 2018). Recent research shows that 62% of dogs consume faeces daily, whereas 38% of dogs eat poo weekly (Hart *et al.*, 2018). There are many assumptions, both medical and behavioural, as to what causes this common behaviour in dogs. However, few are known for certain.

8.1 Behavioural explanations to coprophagia

In my opinion, there are always pretty reliable explanations for anything related to animal behaviour right back in the wild with its relatives. So let's begin there. Sure enough, among the relatives—wolves, wild dogs, and other Canidae—it is considered a part of natural scavenging behaviour. By eating poo, the animal aims mainly to nutritionally enrich its diet. Additionally, mothers will lick their puppies' genital regions frequently during the day in order to stimulate defecation, and then proceed to eating their puppies' excrement in an attempt to keep the den clean. It is for this reason that females seem to be more prone to being coprophagic (Hart *et al.*, 2018). It is also for this reason that puppies who engage in coprophagia may actually be mimicking their mother. It is a common behaviour in puppies but one that usually weans off as they grow into adulthood.

An interesting hypothesis that emerged from the research done by Hart *et al.* (2018) was that domestic dogs may have inherited a wolf-like coprophagic instinct. Wolves eat poo within the first few days of its deposition but not after that. They do this because parasite eggs don't usually hatch into infectious larvae for several days, so if they eat it quickly then they manage to keep the land around their living area parasite-free while they themselves remain safe from parasitic infection. Genius really. Coprophagia could, therefore, really just be an ingenious way that our dogs keep their area free of parasites. Should we be encouraging more of it, I wonder?

Coprophagia is a common behaviour in puppies but one that usually weans off as they grow into adulthood.

If puppies have gotten themselves into the habit of eating faeces due to the mere availability of it within their unclean environment, it is more likely that this habit will also continue into adulthood.

Now, let's return to our domestic scenarios. As already mentioned, it is very often the case that puppies may be kept in unclean conditions before finding their way to you. If, either at the breeders, at the petshop, or at the shelter, puppies have gotten themselves into the habit of eating faeces at this young age due to the mere availability of it within their unclean environment, my experience tells me that it is more likely that this habit will also continue into adulthood, and may even extend into the consumption of faeces of other species; cat, human, horse, and tortoise faeces, in particular, are among the... tastiest(!). Cat's poo, due to higher protein content, and human poo, due to a more varied diet are even considered 'delicacies' by most dogs that will make it their mission to seek them out during their walk.

Other behavioural explanations for coprophagy include play and investigative behaviour especially if Pup or Dog is understimulated. In our attempt to eliminate coprophagia, however, this behaviour gets a lot of unnecessary human attention in the form of either disgust or punishment. Consequently, the results are often the opposite of those expected, and it quickly becomes, as a result of human reinforcement, an attention-seeking ploy. Another human mistake, that may either instigate coprophagia or increase it, is the outdated and cruel training practice of punishing Pup by rubbing his nose in his own excrement. These practices are abusive and cause large amounts of confusion and stress for a dog. The only thing you will succeed in by using these outdated methods is to cause a rupture in your relationship before you have even managed to build a bond (see 'Chapter 2: Why punishment is the wrong way to go').

Any condition that leads to a dog becoming hungrier, such as a poor diet or one with fewer calories aimed at weight loss, may trigger sudden coprophagia.

8.2 Acquiring a new preference for poo delicacies

In the case of coprophagia, the medical explanations are more than the behavioural ones. It is very important, therefore, if your dog suddenly begins to engage in coprophagia, that you visit your vet to rule out any medical conditions first, before searching for a behavioural explanation.

Coprophagia can be a dog's attempt to increase the intake of nutrients either because he is on a poor quality diet, he has a general vitamin or mineral deficiency, or because of an underlying medical condition that results in a decrease in absorption of nutrients—such as parasitic overload. Additionally, any condition that leads to a dog becoming hungrier, such as a poor diet or one with fewer calories aimed at weight loss, may trigger sudden coprophagia.

Other factors that may influence and serve to increase the chances that a dog grows up to be coprophagic are breed, and number of dogs in a household (Hart *et al.*, 2018). The study showed that Hounds and Terriers are the breeds most likely to be coprophagic, while Shetland sheepdogs are the worst offenders. Poodles are the least likely to engage in such distasteful behaviour. Multi-dog households are also more prone to raising coprophagic dogs, presumably due to the increased level of competition between the members of the family and the large amounts of poo produced daily (Coren, 2018). 'Greedy', gluttonous dogs are also much more likely to be coprophagic (Hart *et al.*, 2018).

8.3 Treating coprophagia

The most efficient approach to dealing with coprophagia is managing the problem by preventing access to any excrement. If puppies or dogs can't find it, then they won't eat it and therefore the behaviour, as they grow, will fade away. The more they eat, the more learnt and ingrained the behaviour becomes.

You can teach Pup not to eat poo by training him to come to you upon defecation. When you give your puppy access to the outdoors, stay with him and relatively close; a lead will be useful in the beginning, especially if the urge to eat is strong. Stay with Pup until he defecates and then quickly call him to you before he gets the chance to turn around and consume it. As Pup arrives excitedly, swiftly give him a treat and praise him for coming to you. Then, without haste, go and pick up the poo, leaving the area clean. Now, only after you have cleaned the garden, can you leave him alone to play.

If, after soiling, he turns around and sniffs his poo, correct with a correction cue like *"uh uh"*, and gently distract him by using the lead to bring him to you while repeating enthusiastically *"Pup come"*. Pup then should be rewarded with an amazing treat upon arrival. It shouldn't be long before Pup picks up on this and is coming to you *by himself* to be rewarded as soon as he has soiled.

How to stop Pup's coprophagia-in-the-making

- Keep the den, home and garden clean of excrement.
- When you give your puppy access to the outdoors, keep him on a lead and stay close to him.
- As soon as he defecates, before he gets the chance to turn around and consume it, and using the lead to calmly direct him to you while repeating *"Pup come"*, quickly call him to you.
- If, after soiling, he turns around and sniffs his poo, correct with a cue like *"uh uh"*, and then gently distract him by using the lead to bring him to you to be rewarded.
- Upon arrival, swiftly give him a treat and praise for coming to you.
- Without haste, go and pick up the poo, leaving the area clean.
- Now he can play.
- Pup will soon come to you *by himself* to be rewarded as soon as he has soiled.

CHAPTER 9
Epilogue

And so it is that we come to the end of this fascinating journey through canine toilet troubles. We sincerely hope that you have enjoyed reading this book as much as we have enjoyed writing it, and that you have found what you were looking for to help your canine companion. However, by no means has this book come to an end. Every ending is a new beginning and this is certainly true in our case. We believe that this book is the pivotal point between the end of canine toilet madness and the beginning of canine toilet bliss, for both dogs and their humans. Its effect will continue to spread throughout the canine population long after the reading part is over. The goal? Ending the abandonment of dogs due to toilet-related problems. All knowledge needed in order to create this vitally important change is within this book, and now *you* are the possessor of it. Congratulations!

So, why are we so passionate about canine toilet habits? Toilet behavioural problems may seem mundane to some, but our many years of dealing with them has shown us repeatedly that these sorts of issues are *the* most common reason for relinquishment of dogs by their humans. This saddens us to no end, which is why we made it our mission to do something about it by creating this book. But we cannot do it without you. Now that you have all this information at your fingertips, we are counting on you to help us by:

1. Successfully training any new puppy or any newly adopted rescue dog that you come across if the need arises.

2. Rehabilitating your own, your friends', or your clients' dogs that may be exhibiting soiling problems as only a pro with enhanced empathy and knowledge on canine behaviour and psychology would.

3. Responsibly educating other humans on this subject.

Help us spread the word to save as many human-dog relationships as possible. Saving these relationships will undoubtedly translate into the salvation of canine lives, and into the enhancement of the quality of life for the humans involved. It is worth it. There is no bond like the human-dog bond. It is as mutually beneficial to humans as it is to dogs. Our evolutionary history together is evidence of this fact. It is a great shame that the one thing standing in the way of experiencing this bond to its full potential is usually a lack of communication on the human's part. What a shame to miss out on a partnership so magnificent and life-changing. However, as much as the human is likely to miss out on if the relationship fails, it is the dog who is at the greater disadvantage and who will suffer the most. He will most likely end up losing his home—and maybe even a few more after that—due to his 'toilet problem'. Each time, he will experience and build up more and more confusion, stress, and anxiety, while developing lesser and lesser trust in the human race; a race that he depends on for his life. This is, for us, a cause of great significance; a cause worth fighting for and one that we are sure you support. We therefore welcome you on board this mission and wish you the best of luck.

If, after reading this book, you still have an issue with Pup or Dog, please don't be afraid or ashamed to consult an expert. Give your dog the chance he deserves. You won't regret it; he will be forever grateful, and he will make it *his* mission to express this gratitude on a daily basis!

Help us spread the word to save as many human–dog relationships as possible. Saving these relationships will undoubtedly translate into the salvation of canine lives, and into the enhancement of the quality of life for the humans involved. It is worth it.

Tricks and techniques

Having met hundreds of dogs and puppies, we have confronted all sorts of toilet-related problems and difficulties. The following tricks and techniques have helped us overcome most of them, while still keeping our sense of humour, composure and love for the canine society. Browsing through them, you may find valuable techniques to try, or ideas that could trigger your own imagination towards problem-solving your pooch's unique soiling troubles.

APPENDIX B
Self-diagnosis Flow Chart
(primarily for pee)

This diagram shows all the possible toilet-related behavioural problems discussed in this book. In order to figure out which behavioural problem your dog may be suffering from, all you need to do is start at the top—at 'consistent marking in the house'—and work your way down the flow chart. The route you follow will depend on the symptoms your dog is displaying and should lead you to one or more behavioural problems.

This flow chart is mainly related to pee problems only because most house-soiling issues involve pee and not poo. In some cases, however, such as separation anxiety, attention-seeking and incomplete housebreaking, both peeing and pooing can occur. It is very rare that you get only poo, and if so, this is almost always attention-seeking behaviour or fear of pooing outside (if Dog refuses to poo outside). The presence of poo indicates a more serious situation where the animal is exhibiting more anxiety and/or fear (Ballantyne, n.d.).

When diagnosing an older dog, the first thing to do is look back into puppyhood and ask whether he was ever fully housebroken or not. Was there ever a prolonged period when Dog went to the toilet only outside without any indoor accidents? If not, INCOMPLETE HOUSEBREAKING is the main cause, even though it is very likely that the INCOMPLETE HOUSEBREAKING

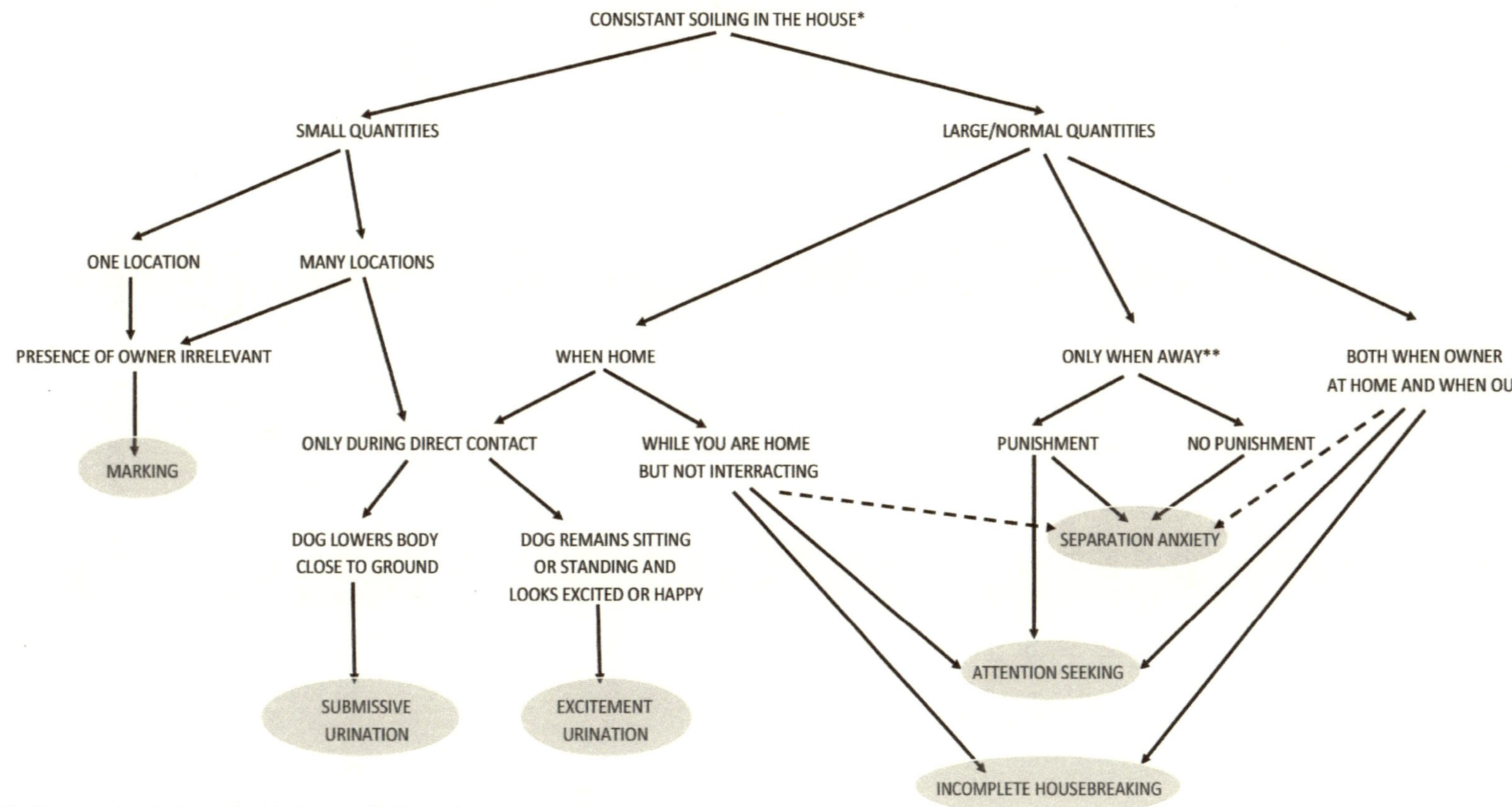

* If soiling started suddenly you should rule out medical issues first

** Relevant if dog is left for a time shorter than his holding capacity

*** Dashed lines indicate that the specific connection/relation/relevance is very rare and holds true only in extreme separation anxiety cases

problem has since evolved into a different behavioural problem, such as:

(1) ATTENTION SEEKING, if punishment was used, or if Dog has somehow managed to get a reaction out of his guardian in the presence of his mess.

(2) MARKING, which can be due to a hormonal influence. Nevertheless, if Dog has never soiled appropriately outside for a prolonged time period, then INCOMPLETE HOUSEBREAKING must be addressed first.

Additionally, don't be alarmed if, when using the Self-diagnosis Flow Chart, you end up with two or more different kinds of behaviour problems, e.g., EXCITEMENT URINATION and SEPARATION ANXIETY. You haven't made a mistake; it can happen. If more than one behavioural problems have been identified, Dog's peeing behaviour is likely multidimensional and therefore more severe, and your best option is to start housetraining from scratch with our INCOMPLETE HOUSEBREAKING PROTOCOL, while also addressing the specific protocols for each behaviour problem that you will find in the relevant sections of this book.

The most significant criteria that you will need to assess in order to successfully self-diagnose Dog's specific peeing problem are:

1. How much pee is Dog depositing? Normal amounts or smaller amounts?

2. Is Dog peeing in one location in the house, i.e., one corner of the house, or many different ones, i.e., different rooms and areas?

3. Is Dog's peeing related to your presence? Does it occur only when you are out, when you are home, or both?

We sincerely hope that you find this flow chart helpful in guiding you towards a pee and poo free home.

References

1. Wells DL and Hepper P (2000). Prevalence of behaviour problems reported by owners of dogs purchased from an animal rescue shelter, *Applied Animal Behaviour Science,* 69(1): 55–65.
2. Salman MD, Hutchison J and Ruch-Gallie R (2000). Behavioral reasons for relinquishment of dogs and cats to 12 shelters, *Journal of Applied Animal Welfare Science,* 3(2): 93–106.
3. New JC Jr, Salman MD, King M, Scarlett JM, Kass PH and Jennifer MH (2000). Characteristics of shelter-relinquished animals and their owners compared with animals and their owners in US pet-owning households, *Journal of Applied Animal Welfare Science,* 3(3): 179–201.
4. Herron ME, Lord LK and Reisner IR (2007). Effects of pre-adoption counseling for owners on house-training success among dogs acquired from shelters, *JAVMA* 231(4): 558–562.
5. Vilà C, Savolainen P, Maldonado J, Amorim I, Rice J, Honeycutt R, Crandall K, Lundenberg J and Wayne R (1997). Multiple and Ancient Origins of the Domestic Dog, *Science,* 276:1687–1689.
6. Leslie S (2018). Is your dog perfect? No?, *Psychology Today*, Available at: https://www.psychologytoday.com/us/blog/decoding-your-pet/201806/is-your-dog-perfect-no.
7. Ballantyne KC (n.d.). Canine house soiling: back to basics, *Today's Veterinary Practice*, Available at:

https://todaysveterinarypractice.com/canine-house-soiling-back-basics.

8. Taylor C, Manganello J, Lee S and Rice CJ (2010). Mothers' spanking of 3-year-old children and subsequent risk of children's aggressive behavior, *Pediatrics*, 125.

9. Stanley C (2011). What are the limits of canine learning?, *Psychology Today*, Available at: https://www.psychologytoday.com/us/blog/canine-corner/201107/what-are-the-limits-canine-learning.

10. Stanley C (2012). Is punishment an effective way to change the behavior of dogs?, *Psychology Today*, Available at:
https://www.psychologytoday.com/us/blog/canine-corner/201205/is-punishment-effective-way-change-the-behavior-dogs.

11. Herron ME, Shofer FS and Reisner IR (2009). Survey of the use and outcome of confrontational and non-confrontational training methods in client-owned dogs showing undesired behaviors, *Applied Animal Behaviour Science*, 117: 47–54.

12. AVSAB (2009). Early puppy socialisation classes: risks vs. benefits, *Veterinary Medicine*, Available at: http://veterinarymedicine.dvm360.com/early-puppy-socialization-classes-weighing-risks-vs-benefits.

13. AVSAB (2008). Position statement on puppy socialisation, Available at:
https://avsab.org/wp-content/uploads/2018/03/Puppy_Socialization_Position_Statement_Download_-_10-3-14.pdf.

14. The APBC Book of Companion Animal Behaviour (2004). 1st Ed, London: Souvenir Press Ltd.

15. Overall K (1997). Clinical Behavioural Medicine for Small Animals, St. Louis, Missouri: Mosby Inc.

16. Arrigo R (2019). Separation anxiety in dogs, *College of Veterinary Medicine Illinois University*, Available at:
https://vetmed.illinois.edu/separation-anxiety-dogs.

17. Dunbar I (2004). Housetraining, Available at:
https://www.dogstardaily.com/files/Housetraining_1.pdf.

18. Overall K (2011). Canine housetraining challenges, Available at:
http://veterinarymedicine.dvm360.com/canine-house-training.

19. Shojai A (2018). Puppy potty accidents: how to clean puppy pee stains. Available at:
https://www.thesprucepets.com/puppy-potty-accidents-2804788.

20. Washington State Department of Health, Dangers of mixing bleach with cleaners, Available at:
https://www.doh.wa.gov/YouandYourFamily/HealthyHome/Contaminants/BleachMixingDangers.

21. Hart BL, Hart LA, Thigpen AP, Tran A and Bain MJ (2018). The paradox of canine conspecific coprophagy, *Veterinary Medicine and Science*, 4(2): 106–114.

22. Coren S (2018). Which dogs eat poop and why do they do it?, *Psychology Today*, Available at:
https://www.psychologytoday.com/us/blog/canine-corner/201801/which-dogs-eat-poop-and-why-do-they-do-it.

Index

Credits

The cover and the general design has been created by Vangelis Karatzas from www.defrost-design.gr.

The dog that pees on the cover and throughout our book is by Levina Anastasia from Shutterstock.com.

The armchair on the cover is by Tribalium from www.gograph.com.

"Lamp post" symbol on pages 18 and 27 is by Jean-Philippe Cabaroc from thenounproject.com.

"Home" symbol on page 24 is by iconixar from thenounproject.com.

The icon on page 25 is an adaptation of "Family" symbol by Luis Prado from thenounproject.com.

"Dog training" symbol (page 29) and "Pet training" symbol (pages 31 and 111) are by ProSymbols from thenounproject.com.

"Angry" symbol on page 32 is by b farias from thenounproject.com.

"Umbrella" symbol on page 34 is by Rflor from thenounproject.com.

The icon on page 36 is an adaptation of "man beating stray dog" symbol by Gan Khoon Lay
from thenounproject.com.

The icon on pages 40 and 103 is an adaptation of "cleaning" symbol by Yeong Rong Kim from thenounproject.com.

"Cleaning" symbol on page 41 is by gzz from thenounproject.com.

"Dog pooping" symbol (pages 45 and 102), "Bed sharing" symbol (pages 106 and 125) and "Dog Clean Up" symbol (page 80) are by Luis Prado from thenounproject.com.

"Dog in a cage" symbol (page 47), "City dog walk" symbol (page 64), "Garden" symbol (pages 67 and 77), "Mover services" symbol (page 114) and "Dog punishment" symbol (page 115) are by Gan Khoon Lay from thenounproject.com.

"Present" symbols on pages 48 and 84 are by Graphic Tigers from thenounproject.com.

"Skyscraper" symbol on page 50 is by Olena Panasovska from thenounproject.com.

"Couch" symbol on page 51 is by Vectors Market from thenounproject.com.

The icon on pages 52 and 91 is an adaptation of "dog pooping" symbol by Luis Prado and "Toilet" symbol by Matthew Davis, both from thenounproject.com.

"Shoes" symbol (pages 53 and 118) and "Crane" symbol (page 90) are by Orin zuu from thenounproject.com.

"Magic" symbol on page 56 is by Olga from thenounproject.com.

The icon on page 57 is an adaptation of "Dog Pee" symbol by Clara Joy and "Pet Carrier" symbol by Luis Prado, both from thenounproject.com.

"Hospital" symbol on page 58 is by IconTrack from thenounproject.com.

"Thinking" symbol on page 59 is by Yamini Ahluwalia from thenounproject.com.

"Brazilwood" symbol on page 60 is by Humberto Cesar Pornaro from thenounproject.com.

"Handcuffs" symbol on page 61 is by P Thanga Vignesh from thenounproject.com.

"Flower" symbol on page 62 is by Andy Mc from thenounproject.com.

The icon on pages 63 and 72 is an adaptation of "grass" symbol by Milinda Courey from thenounproject.com.

"Syringe" symbol on page 65 is by Joel Maynard from thenounproject.com.

The icon on page 68 is an adaptation of "Calendar" symbol by ibrandify from thenounproject.com.

"Dance" symbol on page 71 is by Adrien Duchateau from thenounproject.com.

"Ball" symbol on pages 73, 74, 90 is by Aaaaaammmmiiiiinnnnn from thenounproject.com.

"Alarm Clock" symbol on pages 75 and 123 is by indra anis from thenounproject.com.

"Coat Hanger" symbol on page 78 is by Klea Morianou.

"River" symbol on page 81 is by Daniela Baptista from thenounproject.com.

"Books" symbol on pages 84 and 149 is by Cantasia from thenounproject.com.

"Bracco Italiano", "Airedale Terrier", "Affenpinscher", "Boston Terrier", "Basset Hound", "Akita" symbols on page 89 are by Jenna Foster from thenounproject.com.

"Crocodile" symbol on pages 90 and 108 is by Cédric Villain from thenounproject.com.

"Armchair" symbol on page 90 is by Ben Davis from thenounproject.com.

"TV" symbol on page 90 is by Miza Bintang from thenounproject.com.

"Cat" symbol on page 90 is by Pablo Rozenberg from thenounproject.com.

"Lamp" symbol on page 92 is by By Hrbon from thenounproject.com.

"Angry" symbol on page 94 is by Adrien Coquet from thenounproject.com.

"Toilet" symbol on page 96 is by karina, ID from thenounproject.com.

"Loading files" symbol on page 97 is by Deepz from thenounproject.com.

"Rope" symbol on page 98 is by Valeriy from thenounproject.com.

"Bed" symbol on page 99 is by Muhammad Riza from thenounproject.com.

"Boring" symbol on page 100 is by Phạm Thanh Lộc from thenounproject.com.

"Dog Raincoat" symbol on page 101 is by Llisole from thenounproject.com.

The icon on page 102 is an adaptation of "Ladder" symbol by designvector and "Dog pooping" symbol by Luis Prado from thenounproject.com.

The icon on page 104 is an adaptation of "man beating stray dog" symbol by Gan Khoon Lay and "Greyhound" symbol by Ed Harrison from thenounproject.com.

The icon on page 110 is an adaptation of "Telescope" symbol by Marco Livolsi and "Observation deck" symbol by Jason Gray from thenounproject.com.

"Door" symbol on page 117 is by yanti anis from thenounproject.com.

"Coat" symbol on page 118 is by Creative Stall from thenounproject.com.

"Key" symbol on page 118 is by zidney from thenounproject.com.

"Handbag" symbol on page 118 is by Mohamed Mbarki from thenounproject.com.

"Magic" symbol on page 118 is by Natalia Błaszczyk from thenounproject.com.

The icon on page 119 is an adaptation of "Dog eating" symbol by Luis Prado and "Dog ball" symbol by Willy Roda from thenounproject.com.

"Dog toy" symbol on page 119 is by Willy Roda from thenounproject.com.

"Dog" symbol on page 120 is by Виталий Плут from thenounproject.com.

"Car" symbol on page 121 is by BT Hai from thenounproject.com.

"Sleeping dog" symbol on page 123 is by Amanda Wray from thenounproject.com.

"Begging dog" symbol on page 124 is by Bart Laubsch from thenounproject.com.

The icon on page 129 is an adaptation of "Begging dog" symbol by Bart Laubsch", "Balance" symbol by David, "Parrot" symbol by Em Elvin, "Cat" symbol by Pablo Rozenberg and "Mouse" by Iconic from thenounproject.com.

"Parrot" symbol on page 130 is by Em Elvin from thenounproject.com.

"Rabbit" symbol on page 130 is by parkjisun from thenounproject.com.

"Cat" symbol on page 130 is by Denis Sazhin from thenounproject.com.

"Poop" symbol on page 132 is by Delsart Olivia from thenounproject.com.

The icon on page 133 is an adaptation of "Pet food bowl" symbol by Ken Murray and "Poop" symbol by Icon Island from thenounproject.com.

The icon on page 134 is an adaptation of "Dog" symbol by Yazmin Alanis, "Pet food bowl" symbol by Ken Murray and "Poop" symbol by Icon Island from thenounproject.com.

"Pet" symbol on page 139 is by Lluisa Iborra from thenounproject.com.

Disclaimer

The authors have made every effort to acknowledge copyright holders for material within this publication. Any person who feels they have been overlooked should contact us and we will gladly amend this in future editions.

About the Authors

Marilyn Peters BSc, MSc

Marilyn Peters is a Molecular Biologist (BSc) with a Master's of Science (MSc) in Applied Animal Behaviour and Animal Welfare from the University of Edinburgh, Scotland. Marilyn is no ordinary animal behaviourist, however. She has a unique take on animal behaviour as she combines classical scientific behavioural techniques with a more holistic approach using nutrition, essential oils, flower remedies and energy healing modalities to address the physical, psychological and emotional levels of behavioural dysfunction.

Marilyn is a certified Pet Food Nutrition Specialist both for processed pet foods and raw pet foods alike, and has professional diplomas in:

- Essential oil therapy for animals (Diploma in Animal Psycharomatica) from Nayana Morag of Essential Animals
- Reiki
- EFT (Emotional Freedom Technique Level 1 and 2)
- ThetaHealing (Basic DNA & Advanced DNA, Manifesting and Abundance, Game of Life)
- Tong Ren
- Animal Communication

In 2004, Marilyn returned to Greece and founded Animinds, a consulting business whose mission is to bring humans and animals closer together (find out more about Animinds and Marilyn on her website www.animinds.gr). This mission has set her on a path of extended roleplaying, taking on conventional roles such as animal behaviourist/welfarist, educator, reporter and author, and more unconventional ones such as intuitive, healer, foster mum and volunteer on many different rescue missions.

As important as working hands-on in the field of animal rescue and rehabilitation is, however, education of the public is always top on Marilyn's list of priorities. She strongly believes that only via education will the most fundamental change occur in animal welfare. In doing so, she has been involved in a variety of different animal related programmes and educational events on television, radio and online, both in Greece and abroad. She herself holds many holistic animal behaviour workshops and seminars to educate people about their animals' natural needs and how to communicate with them clearly.

She is currently living in Athens with her husband, two children, four dogs, two cats, rabbit, guinea pig and budgie!

Klea Morianou MArch, MSc

Klea Morianou is an Architect (MArch, National Technical University of Athens) with an MSc in Design & Environmental Analysis from Cornell University. She has a strong background in media on the subject of animal protection legislation, welfare and behaviour. She is the owner of the #1 Greek Source of Pet Information website: TRIHES.GR – Guide to four-legged happiness (www.trihes.gr). She has worked in television as a producer and presenter of the animal welfare TV series Para Triha on SKAI TV (2009-2012), and in journalism as the managing editor of magazines Sky-los & Gata ("Dog & Cat", Kathimerini Publishing, 2011-2013) and GAV ("Woof", Papageorgiou Publishing, 2002-2008). Additionally, she writes articles in magazines and newspapers. She is an active member of the animal welfare groups "Stray.gr", "Zo.Fi.Psy", "Nine-lives-Greece", and was General Secretary of the PFO Animal Welfare Federation (www.pfo.gr). She has rescued and helped rehome hundreds of stray Greek dogs and cats, and has fostered and house-trained dozens of them. At the moment she lives in Athens with her husband, two dogs and 12 cats.

9 7 9 8 6 0 5 5 7 1 3 9 1